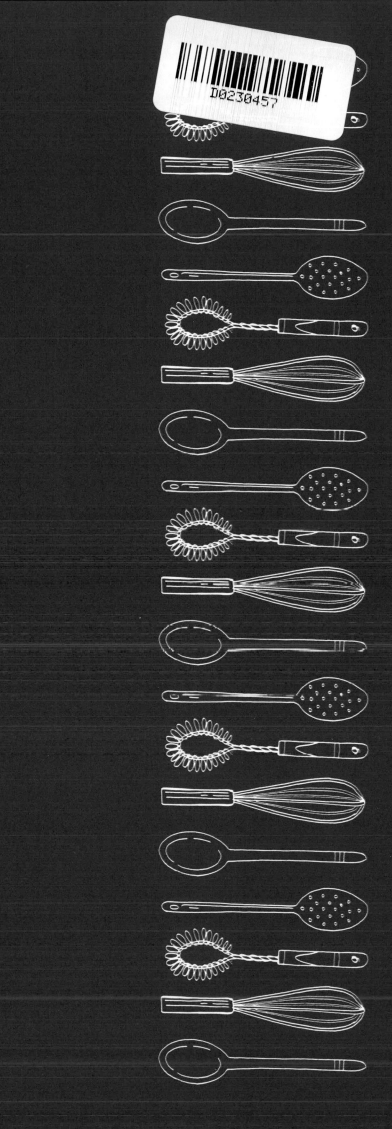

THE LOW CHOLESTEROL COOKBOOK

THE LOW CHOLESTEROL COOKBOOK

OVER 50 RECIPES, EACH ONE LOW IN CHOLESTEROL AND SATURATED FATS, BUT HIGH IN TASTE AND APPEAL

CONSULTANT EDITOR
CHRISTINE FRANCE

PREMIER

This edition first published in 1998 by Lorenz Books

© Anness Publishing Limited 1998

Lorenz Books is an imprint of
Anness Publishing Limited
Hermes House
88–89 Blackfriars Road
London SE1 8HA

ISBN 1 85967 574 3

A CIP catalogue record for this book is available from the British Library

Publisher: Joanna Lorenz
Senior Cookery Editor: Linda Fraser
Editor: Margaret Malone
Designer: Sara Kidd
Introduction: Christine McFadden
Nutritional Analysis: Wendy Doyle
Photography: Karl Adamson, Edward Allwright, Steve Baxter, James Duncan,
Amanda Heywood, Don Last, Patrick McLeavey, Michael Michaels,
Thomas Odulate and Peter Reilly
Recipes: Catherine Atkinson, Carla Capalbo, Kit Chan, Roz Denny, Christine
France, Shirley Gill, Christine Ingram, Sue Maggs, Annie Nichols, Maggie
Pannell, Laura Washburn and Stephen Wheeler

Printed and bound in Singapore

Most of the recipes in this book have previously appeared in
The Ultimate Low Cholesterol, Low Fat Cookbook

1 3 5 7 9 10 8 6 4 2

NOTES
For all recipes, quantities are given in both metric and imperial measures and,
where appropriate, measures are also given in standard cups and spoons.
Follow one set, but not a mixture, because they are not interchangeable.

Standard spoon and cup measures are level.
1 tsp = 5ml, 1 tbsp = 15ml, 1 cup = 250ml/8fl oz

Australian standard tablespoons are 20ml. Australian readers should
use 3 tsp in place of 1 tbsp for measuring small quantities of gelatine,
cornflour, salt, etc.

Size 3 medium eggs are used unless otherwise stated.

CONTENTS

INTRODUCTION

Cooking and eating good food are among life's greatest pleasures. Unfortunately, the foods we tend to enjoy most are often fatty, and certain types of fat raise the level of blood cholesterol – a substance strongly implicated in heart disease, stroke and high blood pressure.

Cholesterol is found in the cells of humans and animals, and in the food we eat. Body cholesterol is manufactured in the liver and is used to carry essential fatty acids around the bloodstream to various organs. The body makes all the cholesterol it needs and any excess accumulates on the walls of the arteries and then restricts the passage of blood and oxygen to the heart. This is why a high level of cholesterol in the blood is generally recognized as one of the risk factors in the development of heart disease.

Dietary cholesterol is found in saturated fats and in food derived from animals – meat, offal, egg yolk and dairy produce, for instance. Fats derived from vegetables are cholesterol-free. Interestingly, although some low-fat foods such as prawns contain high levels of cholesterol, it seems that blood cholesterol levels are more affected by the amount of saturated fat in the diet than the amount of cholesterol. So it's now thought that prawns and other shellfish do not greatly increase cholesterol levels even though they contain cholesterol themselves.

Above: Delicious fruit and vegetables – the perfect start to a healthy diet.

When we eat more saturated fat than we need, the body increases cholesterol production and the excess ends up in the bloodstream. So even a low-cholesterol diet can raise your blood cholesterol if saturated fats aren't reduced as well.

Most of us eat fats in one form or another every day. In fact, we need to consume a small amount to maintain a healthy and balanced diet, but almost everyone – not just the cholesterol-conscious – can afford to, and should, reduce their fat intake, particularly of saturated fats.

By choosing the right types of fat and making small, simple changes to the way you cook and prepare food, you can reduce your overall fat intake quite dramatically and enjoy a low-fat, low cholesterol diet without really noticing any difference.

As you will see, watching your fat and cholesterol intake doesn't necessarily mean dieting and deprivation. *The Low Cholesterol Cookbook* contains an introduction explaining all you need to know about basic healthy eating. There are instructions on how to cook with fat-free and low-fat ingredients; suggestions about which foods to cut down on and what to try instead; information on the best cookware available and a comprehensive fat and calorie content chart.

Here are over 50 easy-to-follow recipes that your whole family can enjoy. Every recipe has been developed in line with modern nutritional guide-lines, and each one has at-a-glance nutritional information so you can instantly check the calorie, saturated fat and cholesterol content. The selection of foods included will surprise you: pizza and pastas, tasty sautés and stews, vegetable main courses and salads, fish and seafood dishes galore and delicious breads, biscuits and cakes – all with less fat than traditional recipes, of course, but packed with flavour and vitality.

Below: Be aware not only of what you eat, but how much you eat of each of the five main food groups.

THE IMPORTANCE OF DIET

A healthy diet is one that provides the body with all the nutrients it needs for growth and repair and to resist disease. To get the balance right, it is important to know just how much to eat of each type of food.

Of the five main food groups (see below), it is recommended that we eat at least five portions of fruit and vegetables a day (excluding potatoes). We should also eat a high proportion of energy-producing foods such as cereals, pasta, rice, beans, bread and potatoes; moderate amounts of meat, fish, poultry, eggs and dairy products; and only small amounts of fat and sugar.

THE FIVE MAIN FOOD GROUPS

● Fruit and vegetables
● Cereals, rice, potatoes, beans, bread and pasta
● Meat, poultry, fish and eggs
● Milk and other dairy foods
● Fats, oils and sugars

You can reduce your intake of dietary cholesterol by cutting down on fat, particularly the saturated kind. Aim to limit your daily fat intake to no more than 30 per cent of total calories. In real terms, this means that for an average daily intake of 2000 calories, 30 per cent of energy would come from 600 calories. Since each gram of fat provides 9 calories, your total daily intake should be no more than 66.6g fat. Of this amount no more than 10 per cent (that is 6.6g) should consist of saturated fat.

TYPES OF FAT

All fats and oils are made up of three units of fatty acids and a unit of glycerol (glycerine). Their individual properties vary according to the type and combination of fatty acids.

All fatty acids are made up of chains of carbon atoms, some or all of which have either one or two hydrogen atoms

Above: Though not all fats are 'bad', only small amounts are needed in the diet.

attached to them. If any of the hydrogen atoms are missing, two carbon atoms join together to form what is known as a double bond. Fatty acids containing double bonds are said to be unsaturated. Fatty acids containing more than one double bond are called polyunsaturated, while those with a single double bond are known as monounsaturated. Those containing all the hydrogen atoms they can hold are called saturated fatty acids.

All fats contain both saturated and unsaturated (either poly- or monounsaturated) fatty acids, but if the proportion of saturated is greater than unsaturated, the fat is generally said to be 'saturated', and vice versa.

● *Saturated fats –*
Saturated fats are generally solid at room temperature and are mostly found in foods derived from animal sources. However, there are also saturated fats of vegetable origin, notably coconut and palm oils (although these do not contain cholesterol), as well as certain margarines and oils in which some of the unsaturated fatty acids have been processed into saturated ones. These products are labelled 'hydrogenated' and are best avoided.

● *Polyunsaturated fats –*
Polyunsaturated fats are usually liquid at room temperature. There are two types: those of vegetable or plant origin (containing fatty acids known as omega 6), such as nut, seed and vegetable oils, and soft margarine; and those from oily fish (omega 3), such as herring and sardines. Small quantities are essential for good health, and ideally we should consume equal amounts of omega 6 and omega 3 oils. Most of us need to boost our omega 3 intake.

● *Monounsaturated fats –*
Monounsaturated fats are found in foods such as olive oil and rapeseed oil, some nuts such as almonds and walnuts, oily fish and avocado pears. These fats are thought to help reduce blood cholesterol levels, and could explain why there is a low incidence of heart disease in Mediterranean countries where they are a major part of the diet.

CHOLESTEROL

Although usually associated with fats, cholesterol isn't actually a fat itself; it is a white, waxy material belonging to a group of substances known as lipoproteins. Cholesterol travels round the bloodstream in tiny droplets of lipoprotein, of which there are three densities: very low density lipoproteins (VLDL), low density (LDL) and high density (HDL). When you eat a lot of saturated fats, your liver produces huge quantities of VLDLs and LDLs. Both types are rich in cholesterol and are the culprits when it comes to blocked arteries. HDLs, however, are thought to help prevent clogged arteries. This is why HDLs are sometimes referred to as 'good' and LDLs as 'bad'.

The recommended maximum daily intake of cholesterol is 300mg. This may seem a lot, but it's very easy to exceed the limit if your diet contains high-cholesterol foods (see box).

CUTTING DOWN ON FAT

About one quarter of the fat we eat comes from meat and meat products, one-fifth from dairy products and margarine, and the rest from cakes, biscuits, pastries and other foods. There are also 'hidden' fats in foods such as many nuts, hummus, avocado.

By being aware of high-fat foods and the type of fat in them, and by making simple changes to your eating habits, you can reduce quite considerably the total fat content of your diet, and therefore control cholesterol levels.

BOOSTING FIBRE

Studies have shown that certain types of fibre can help reduce blood cholesterol and restrict fat absorption. There are about six different types of fibre and these can be divided into two groups: soluble and insoluble.

Soluble fibre contains pectin, which acts as a binding agent, helping prevent cholesterol from being absorbed. As a result, the liver's store of cholesterol becomes depleted and it takes up cholesterol from the bloodstream, lowering the levels. Foods containing soluble fibre include oats, buckwheat, beans, apples and dried fruit.

Insoluble fibre is made up of cellulose (found in all plant foods) and lignin (a woody substance found in the central core of fibrous vegetables such as old carrots and parsnips).

Unlike most celluloses, lignin helps lower blood cholesterol by binding to bile acids, whose function is to emulsify fat, thus increasing their excretion from the body.

BOOSTING ANTIOXIDANTS

Our body cells can be damaged by destructive molecules known as free radicals. The process is called oxidation and is similar to the type of reaction

CHOLESTEROL CONTENT OF SELECTED FOODS	
	mg cholesterol per 100g
Lambs' brains	2200
Egg yolk	1260
Herring roe	575
Whole egg	450
Calves' liver	370
Lambs' kidneys	315
Caviar (bottled)	285
Mayonnaise	260
Butter	230
Squid	225
Prawns	195
Double cream	140
Pork	110
Salami	79
Lamb, lean	74
Chicken, light meat	70
Cheddar cheese	70
Trout	70
Pork, lean	63
Beef, lean	58
Haddock	36

that causes rust in metal when exposed to the oxygen in the air. Some scientists now believe that oxidized fat and cholesterol may be linked to some cancers. Antioxidants provide powerful protection by destroying free radicals, and are also thought to prevent 'bad' LDL cholesterol from oxidizing and causing damage to the artery walls.

The main antioxidants are the carotenes (the plant form of vitamin A) found in orange-fleshed fruit and vegetables; vitamin C found in citrus fruit and many other fruits and vege-tables; vitamin E found in vegetable oils, seeds and nuts; the minerals selenium, zinc and magnesium; and certain proteins found in cabbages as well as other fruits and vegetables.

Left: Beware of those foods that are high in cholesterol, such as meat and meat products, cream and cheese.

KEY CHOLESTEROL-LOWERING FOODS

Try to include the following foods in your daily diet. They all help lower 'bad' LDL cholesterol, which can clog the arteries or oxidize, causing damage to the artery walls. These foods also boost 'good' HDL cholesterol, which removes LDL cholesterol from the bloodstream.

● *Fish* – Oily fish, such as mackerel, sardines, herring, trout and salmon, contain valuable fatty acids known as omega 3. These fatty acids boost HDL cholesterol and are strongly believed to help prevent heart disease. Try to eat oily fish 2–3 times a week. Grill or bake in the oven without any extra oil. Sprinkle with lemon or lime juice and chopped fresh herbs.

● *Nuts* – Although nuts are high in fat, it's the monounsaturated kind that lowers 'bad' LDL cholesterol and discourages it from oxidizing and damaging the artery walls. Nuts are also a valuable source of vitamin E, which protects against oxidative damage. Almonds and walnuts are said to be particularly effective. Eat just a few nuts each day as a snack, or add them to salads or cakes.

● *Oats* – Just 50g/2oz of oats or oat bran a day, as part of a low-fat diet, is known to dramatically reduce blood cholesterol. As well as eating oats in porridge and muesli, add them to home-made bread and biscuits, or sprinkle into crumble mixtures. Sprinkle oat bran over yogurt or fruit and sweeten with a little honey.

● *Olive oil and rapeseed oil* – These oils, particularly olive oil, are very high in monounsaturates, which lower 'bad' LDL cholesterol and prevent it from causing oxidative damage to the arteries. They slightly raise or keep 'good' HDL cholesterol the same. Polyunsaturated oils such as sunflower and corn oil lower both types of cholesterol, so you miss out on the protective power of HDL cholesterol. Use 'pure' olive oil in moderation for cooking and 'extra virgin' for salads.

● *Pulses* – Countless studies indicate that pulses – dried beans, lentils and chick-peas – work miracles in fighting high cholesterol when eaten on a daily basis. You can use all types of beans: kidney, pinto, flageolet, butter beans, haricot, soya – even ordinary baked beans. Use tinned or precooked pulses to replace some or all of the meat in stews; add cooked pulses to gutsy salads and soups; or whizz them in a blender with garlic, lemon, herbs and a little olive oil to make dips and pâtés.

Below: Certain foods boost 'good' cholesterol while reducing the 'bad'.

FRESH FRUIT AND VEGETABLES

Including plenty of fruit and vegetables in your diet – ideally at least five portions daily (excluding potatoes) – will help control blood cholesterol levels. Almost all are naturally fat-free as well as providing carotene (the plant form of vitamin A), vitamins C and E, minerals and dietary fibre.

Apples – A useful source of energy-giving carbohydrate, vitamin C and pectin (a soluble fibre thought to lower blood cholesterol).

Apricots – An excellent source of carotene and cholesterol-lowering soluble fibre.

Bananas – Packed with carbohydrate, bananas are a fat-free energy booster. Add to yogurt, breakfast cereal and muesli, or spread on wholemeal toast.

Citrus fruit – An excellent source of vitamin C and carotene (antioxidants that may help minimize the risk of heart disease). Pectin in the flesh and fibrous membranes is thought to help lower blood cholesterol.

Grapes – Red and black grapes are rich in bioflavonoids (antioxidants that may help protect against heart disease and some cancers).

Kiwi fruit – Kiwis are an excellent source of vitamin C and also provide pectin, a cholesterol-lowering soluble fibre.

Mangoes – Wonderful mixed with yogurt or in a tropical fruit salad, mangoes are packed with beta carotene, vitamin C and soluble fibre.

Prunes – Prunes contain masses of pectin, a soluble fibre that accounts for their laxative effect. Pectin also helps lower blood cholesterol levels.

Strawberries – Rich in vitamin C and soluble and insoluble fibre that help remove cholesterol from the blood.

Asparagus – An excellent source of beta carotene and a useful source of vitamins C and E (all natural antioxidants, which may help lower blood cholesterol).

Above: Eating plenty of fruit and vegetables nowadays is a treat, not a punishment!

Avocados – Rich in monounsaturates thought to restrict damage caused to arteries by 'bad' LDL cholesterol. A good source of vitamin E – a powerful antioxidant – and may be included in a low-fat diet in moderation. Serve with a fat-free dressing.

Broccoli – Probably topping the list of disease fighting vegetables, broccoli is an excellent source of antioxidants carotene, vitamins C and E and cholesterol-lowering soluble fibre.

Carrots – A fantastic source of beta carotene, a powerful antioxidant that protects the arteries against damage by 'bad' LDL cholesterol. Very rich in cholesterol-lowering soluble fibre.

Garlic – An all-round miracle vegetable, strongly believed to thin the blood and reduce blood cholesterol. Use raw in salad dressings, roast whole heads and eat with a selection of roasted vegetables, or sauté gently in stir-fries, sauces and stews.

Kale – A rich source of antioxidant vitamins, which help protect against 'bad' LDL cholesterol. Tender baby kale can be microwaved or used raw in salads.

Mushrooms – Sweat in a little stock rather than butter or slice and use raw in salads. Eaten daily, Asian shiitake mushrooms are thought to help reduce blood cholesterol levels and high blood pressure.

Onions – Onions are an exceptionally powerful antioxidant and strongly believed to thin the blood and lower cholesterol. An essential flavouring for many savoury dishes; serve them cooked or raw in salads, or baked as a vegetable in their own right.

Parsnips – A tasty root vegetable rich in cholesterol-lowering soluble fibre. Eat them baked, mashed or grated raw in salads.

Potatoes – Provide energy-giving carbohydrate, vitamin C and soluble fibre, but are frequently prepared using high-fat cooking methods such as roasting and frying. Boil, steam or bake potatoes instead, and serve with low-fat dressings.

Sweet peppers – An excellent source of beta carotene and vitamin C, which help reduce damage caused by 'bad' LDL cholesterol. Use raw in salads, add to stir-fries, roast in the oven and add to soups, stews and sauces.

COOKING WITH LOW-FAT AND FAT-FREE INGREDIENTS

Nowadays many foods are available in reduced-fat or very low-fat versions. In every supermarket you'll find a huge array of low-fat dairy products such as reduced-fat milks and cream, yogurt, hard and soft cheeses and fromage frais. There is also an increasing variety of reduced-fat sweet or chocolate biscuits; reduced-fat or fat-free salad dressings and mayonnaise; reduced-fat crisps and snacks; low-fat, half-fat and very low-fat spreads; and even reduced-fat ready-made meals.

Other foods, such as fresh fruit and vegetables, pasta, rice, potatoes and bread, naturally contain very little fat and they help reduce blood cholesterol levels. Some foods such as soy sauce, wine, vinegar, cider, sherry and honey contain no fat at all. By combining these and other low-fat foods with low fat cooking techniques, you can create delicious dishes that contain very little fat.

Some low-fat or reduced-fat ingredients and products work better than others in cooking, but often a simple substitution of one for another will produce good results.

LOW-FAT SPREADS IN COOKING

There is a huge variety of low-fat, reduced-fat and half-fat spreads available in our supermarkets. Some are suitable for cooking, while others are best used only for spreading.

Generally speaking, the very low-fat spreads with a fat content of around 20 per cent or less have a high water content, which will evaporate on heating making them unsuitable for cooking and better for spreading only.

Clockwise from left: olive oil, sunflower oil, buttermilk blend, sunflower light, olive oil reduced-fat spread, reduced-fat butter and (centre) very low-fat spread.

Low-fat or half-fat spreads with a fat content of around 40 per cent are suitable for spreading and can be used for some cooking methods. They are suitable for recipes such as all-in-one cake and biscuit recipes, all-in-one sauce recipes, sautéing vegetables over a low heat, choux pastry and some cake icings.

When these low-fat spreads are used for cooking, they may behave slightly differently from full-fat products such as butter or margarine. With some recipes, the cooked result may be slightly different from that produced by the traditional method, but will still be very acceptable. Other recipes will be just as tasty and successful. For example, choux pastry made using half- or low-fat spread is often slightly crisper and lighter in texture than traditional choux pastry and a cheesecake biscuit base made with melted half- or low-fat spread combined with crushed biscuit crumbs may be slightly softer in texture and less crispy than a biscuit base made using melted butter.

LOW-FAT AND VERY LOW-FAT SNACKS

Instead of reaching for a packet of crisps, a high-fat biscuit or a chocolate bar when hunger strikes, choose one of these tasty low-fat snacks to fill that hungry hole.

● A piece of fresh fruit or vegetable such as an apple, banana or carrot is delicious, easy to eat and will also increase soluble fibre and help lower blood cholesterol. Keep chunks or sticks wrapped in a polythene bag in the refrigerator. If you like, skewer fruit pieces on to cocktail sticks or short bamboo skewers to make them into mini kebabs.

● Crackers, such as water biscuits or crispbreads, spread with reduced-sugar jam or marmalade.

● Instead of cream, dollop some very low-fat plain or fruit yogurt or even fromage frais on to puddings.

● Toasted crumpet spread with yeast extract.

● A bowl of wholewheat breakfast cereal or no-added-sugar muesli served with a little skimmed milk. Oats are one of the best cereals for reducing blood cholesterol.

● A portion of canned fruit in natural fruit juice – serve with a spoonful or two of fat-free yogurt.

● One or two crisp rice cakes or oat cakes – delicious on their own, or topped with honey, or reduced-fat cheese. Oats are well-known for their cholesterol-lowering properties.

● A handful of dried fruit such as raisins, apricots or sultanas will help lower blood cholesterol. These also make a perfect addition to children's packed lunches or school break snacks.

When heating half- or low-fat spreads, never cook them over a high heat. Always use a heavy-based pan over a low heat to avoid burning, spitting or spoiling, and stir all the time. With all-in-one sauces, the mixture should be whisked continuously over a low heat.

Half-fat or low-fat spreads are not suitable for shallow or deep-fat frying, pastry making, rich fruit cakes, some biscuits, shortbread, in place of clarified butter or preserves such as lemon curd. Remember also, that the keeping qualities of recipes made using half- or low-fat spreads may be reduced slightly, because of the lower fat content of those spreads.

Another way to reduce the fat content of recipes, particularly cake recipes, is to use a dried fruit purée in place of all or some of the fat in a recipe. By using dried fruit, you'll also be increasing your intake of soluble fibre, which, in turn, helps reduce blood cholesterol levels. Many cake recipes work well using dried fruit purée, but other recipes may not be so successful. Pastry does not work well, for instance. Breads work very well – perhaps because the amount of fat is usually small – as do some biscuits and bars, such as brownies and flapjacks.

To make a dried fruit purée to use in recipes, chop 115g/4oz ready-to-eat dried fruit and place in a blender or food processor with 75ml/5 tbsp water and blend to a roughly smooth purée. Then simply substitute the same weight of this dried fruit purée for all or just some of the amount of fat in the recipe. The purée will keep in the refrigerator for up to three days.

You can use prunes, dried apricots, dried peaches or dried apples, or substitute mashed fresh fruit, such as ripe bananas or lightly cooked apples, without the added water.

EASY WAYS TO CUT DOWN ON FAT

There are lots of simple, no-fuss ways of reducing fat in your daily diet. Just follow the simple 'eat less – try instead' suggestions to discover how easy it is.

Eat less – Butter, margarine and hard fats.

● *Try instead* – When baking chicken or fish, rather than adding a knob of butter, try wrapping the food in a loosely sealed parcel of foil or greaseproof paper and adding some wine or fruit juice and herbs or spices to the food before sealing the parcel.
● Where possible, use low- and very low-fat spreads, or non-hydrogenated vegetable margarine.

Eat less – Fatty meats and high-fat products such as meat pâtés, pies and sausages.

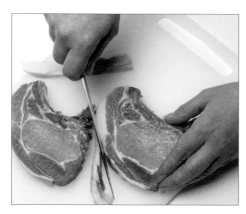

● *Try instead* – Low-fat meats such as chicken and turkey. Cut off any visible fat and skin before cooking.

● Eat fish more often. White fish is practically fat-free and oily fish contains cholesterol-lowering fatty acids.
● Make gravies using vegetable water or fat-free stock rather than using meat juices.

Eat less – Fried foods.
● *Try instead* – Fat-free cooking methods such as grilling, microwaving, steaming or baking whenever possible.
● When grilling foods, the addition of fat is often unnecessary. If the food shows signs of drying, you can lightly brush it with a small amount of monounsaturated oil such as rapeseed or olive oil.
● Steaming or boiling are easy fat-free ways of cooking many foods, especially vegetables, fish and chicken.

● Try cooking in a non-stick wok with only a very small amount of oil.

Eat less – Hard cooking fats such as lard or hard margarine, and polyunsaturated oil such as corn, safflower and sunflower oils. These oils are easily oxidized and may cause 'bad' LDL cholesterol to become toxic.
● *Try instead* – Monounsaturated oils such as olive and rapeseed oils. These protect the arteries by reducing 'bad' LDL cholesterol without lowering the level of 'good' HDL cholesterol.
● Microwaved and grilled foods rarely need the addition of fat, so add herbs or spices for extra flavour.

Eat less – Added fat in cooking.
● *Try instead* – To cook with little or no fat. Use heavy-based or good-quality non-stick pans, so that the food doesn't stick.
● Try using a small amount of spray oil in cooking to control exactly how much fat you are using.

● Always roast or grill meat or poultry on a rack.
● Choose heavy-based or good-quality cookware; you'll find that the amount of fat needed for cooking foods can be kept to an absolute minimum. When making casseroles or meat sauces such as bolognese, dry-fry the meat to brown it and then drain off all the excess fat before adding the other ingredients. If you do need a little fat, choose an oil that is high in mono-unsaturates such as olive or rapeseed oil and always use as little as possible.

● Use fat-free or low-fat ingredients for cooking, such as fruit juice, low-fat or fat-free stock, wine or even beer.

● When serving vegetables such as boiled potatoes, carrots or peas, resist the temptation to add a knob of butter or margarine. Instead, sprinkle with chopped fresh herbs, freshly ground spices, lemon juice or soy sauce.

● Try poaching foods such as chicken or fish in stock.

● Sauté vegetables in wine, fruit juice or low-fat or fat-free stock.

● Marinate meat or poultry in mixtures of alcohol, herbs or spices, and vinegar or fruit juice. This will help to tenderize the meat, as well as adding flavour and colour and can be used for basting during cooking.

● Cook vegetables in a covered saucepan over a low heat with a little water so they cook in their own juices.

● Try braising vegetables in the oven in wine, low-fat or fat-free stock, or even water with the addition of some herbs.

● Poach fruit in wine for a quick, low-fat dessert. Serve with a dollop of fresh yoghurt instead of cream.

Eat less – Eggs, which are high in both saturated fat and cholesterol. Limit intake to no more than 3 or 4 a week.

● *Try instead* – Egg whites in recipes calling for whole eggs. Limit egg yolks to 1 per serving when making scrambled eggs. For something a little different, make mayonnaise with tofu instead of egg yolks.

Eat less – Rich creamy, salad dressings, such as full-fat mayonnaise, French or Thousand Island.

● *Try instead* – Reduced-fat or fat-free mayonnaise or dressings. Make salad dressings at home with low-fat yogurt or fromage frais, or blender-whipped cottage cheese, ricotta or buttermilk in recipes calling for soured cream or mayonnaise.

● Try lemon juice, soy sauce and fresh herbs on salads – quick and easy but also full of flavour.

Eat less – Full-fat dairy products such as whole milk, cream, butter, hard margarine, crème fraîche, whole-milk yogurts and hard cheese.

● *Try instead* – Semi-skimmed or skimmed milk, low-fat yogurts, low-fat fromage frais and low- and reduced fat cheeses, such as Cheddar, and reduced-fat creams and crème fraîche.

● Beware of dried skimmed milk and coffee creamers – these may be skimmed of animal fat, but may have vegetable fat added.

Eat less – High-fat snacks such as crisps, tortilla chips, fried snacks and pastries, chocolate cakes, muffins, doughnuts, sweet pastries and biscuits – especially chocolate ones!

● *Try instead* – Low-fat and fat-free fresh or dried fruits, breadsticks or vegetable sticks.

● Make your own low-fat cakes, biscuits and breads.

● If you do buy ready-made cakes and biscuits, always choose low-fat and reduced-fat versions.

● Dried fruits are a traditional addition to cakes and quick breads and there is a very wide range available, from banana to apricots and mango. The natural sugars add sweetness to baked goods and keep them moist, making it possible to use less fat.

● Use good-quality bakeware that doesn't need greasing before use.

● If you do have to grease your bakeware, use non-stick baking paper and grease only lightly before lining.

HOW TO REDUCE OIL IN COOKING

For fat-free or low-fat cooking it's best to avoid roasting and frying as they can increase the fat content of food. Instead poach, grill, bake, steam or microwave food, all successful ways of cooking without adding fat. Below are some further clever techniques that may be used for reducing or eliminating the amount of oil used in cooking.

SWEATING VEGETABLES

GOOD FOR: pan-frying vegetables such as onions, mushrooms, carrots and celery, which would usually be initially fried in oil or butter, as the basis of many savoury recipes.

HOW TO: Put the sliced vegetables into a non-stick frying pan with about 150ml/¼ pint/⅔ cup light stock. Cook for 5 minutes or until the vegetables are tender and the stock has reduced. Add 15ml/1 tbsp dry wine or wine vinegar for a little piquancy and continue cooking for a further few minutes until the vegetables are lightly browned.

MARINATING

GOOD FOR: Adding flavour as well as helping to tenderize and keep the food moist during cooking without adding any fat. Useful for meat, fish, poultry and vegetables. The marinade may also be used for basting or it can be added to an accompanying sauce.

HOW TO: Wine, soy sauce, vinegar, citrus juices and yogurt all make excellent fat-free marinade bases with herbs and spices added for extra flavour. Leave fish for 1 hour, marinate meat and poultry overnight if possible.

PARCEL COOKING

GOOD FOR: Fish, chicken, vegetables and fruit, allowing the food to cook in its own juices and the steam created, holding in all the flavour and nutrient value and eliminating the need for oil or fats.

HOW TO: Enclose food in individual foil or greaseproof parcels and add extra flavourings, such as a little wine, herbs and spices, if liked. Twist or fold the parcel ends to secure and ensure that the juices can't run out, then either bake, steam or, if using foil, cook on a barbecue.

SEARING

GOOD FOR: Sealing the juices into meat and poultry. Even lean cuts trimmed of skin and visible fat contain some hidden fat, so adding extra fat isn't necessary.

HOW TO: Place the meat in a heavy-based pan over moderate heat and brown evenly on all sides. If the meat sticks slightly, remove from the pan, brush or spray a little olive oil on to the pan's surface, heat, then return the meat to the pan. Drain off any excess fat that comes out of the meat.

LOW-FAT SAUCES

Sauces can introduce an unwelcome amount of fat into a recipe so that naturally low-fat foods like vegetables, white fish and skinless chicken may end up being served in a rich, high-fat coating. However, by following the tips and techniques below, it's easy to adapt such sauces without sacrificing flavour and appeal.

BÉARNAISE SAUCE

Some fat savings can be made to this classic piquant sauce by using a small amount of butter and fewer egg yolks.

INGREDIENTS

Makes 350ml/³/4 pint/1¹/2 cups
150ml/ ¹/4 pint/²/3 cup white wine
60ml/4 tbsp white wine vinegar
15ml/1 tbsp finely chopped shallot
15ml/1 tbsp cornflour
175ml/6fl oz/³/4 cup water
2 egg yolks, lightly beaten
40g/1¹/2oz/3 tbsp unsalted butter, melted
15ml/1 tbsp chopped fresh tarragon
15ml/1 tbsp chopped fresh parsley
salt and black pepper

1 Put the wine, vinegar, shallot and freshly ground black pepper in a saucepan. Bring to the boil and simmer until reduced to 30–45ml/2–3 tbsp. Strain, discarding solids.

2 Put the cornflour and water in a bowl over a pan of gently simmering water. Whisk for 3–4 minutes until thickened. Stir in the vinegar mixture. Remove from the heat, whisk in the egg yolks and half the butter. Place over the hot water again and stir constantly for 3–4 minutes until thickened.

3 Add the chopped herbs. Whisk in the remaining butter and salt to taste. Use immediately.

EGG-FREE MAYONNAISE

Egg yolks are high in cholesterol and contain saturated fat. Here's a way of making mayonnaise without them.

INGREDIENTS

Makes 250ml/¹/2 pint/1 cup
100g/4oz firm tofu, drained and pressed dry
60ml/4 tbsp 'light' Greek yogurt or low-fat fromage frais
30ml/2 tbsp white wine or vinegar
5ml/1 tsp sea salt
75ml/5 tbsp olive oil
black pepper

Put the tofu, yogurt or fromage frais, wine or vinegar and salt in a blender and process for 2–3 minutes until very smooth. With the blender running, add the oil a little at a time, until the mixture thickens. Season. Use immediately.

OIL-FREE DRESSINGS

Whisk together 90ml/6 tbsp low-fat natural yogurt, 30ml/2 tbsp lemon juice and season to taste with freshly ground black pepper. If you prefer, wine, cider or fruit vinegar or even orange juice could be used in place of the lemon juice. Add chopped fresh herbs, crushed garlic, mustard, honey, or other flavourings, if you like.

VEGETABLE PURÉE

Many recipes for sauces are traditionally thickened by adding cream, beurre manié (a butter and flour paste) or egg yolks, all of which add saturated fat and cholesterol to the sauce. If cooked vegetables are included in the recipe, blend some down in a food processor to make a purée, then stir back into the juices to produce a thickened sauce. Good for casserole sauces.

THREE WAYS TO MAKE LOW-FAT SAUCES

The traditional roux method for making a sauce won't work successfully if using a low-fat spread. This is because of the high water content, which will evaporate on heating, leaving insufficient fat to blend with the flour. However, below are three quick and easy low-fat alternatives.

1 The all-in-one method: Place 25g/1oz/2 tbsp each of low-fat spread and plain flour in a pan with 300ml/¹/2 pint/1¹/4 cups skimmed milk. Bring to the boil, whisking continuously until thickened and smooth.

2 Using stock to replace fat: Sweat cut-up vegetables, such as onions and mushrooms, in a small amount of stock in a non-stick pan rather than frying in fat.

3 Using cornflour to thicken: Blend 15ml/1 tbsp cornflour with 15–30ml/1–2 tbsp cold water, then whisk into 300ml/¹/2 pint/1¹/4 cups simmering stock or milk, bring to the boil and cook for 1 minute, stirring continuously.

LOW-FAT STOCKS

A good stock is invaluable in the kitchen. The most delicious soups, stews, casseroles and sauces rely on a good home-made stock for success. Neither a stock cube nor a canned consommé will do if you want the best flavour.

Simple and economical to make, below are three easy-to-follow recipes for low-fat chicken, meat and vegetable stock. Keep in the refrigerator for 4 days, or freeze for up to 6 months for meat and poultry, 1 month for the vegetable.

LOW-FAT CHICKEN STOCK

─── INGREDIENTS ───

Makes 1.5 litres/2½ pints/6¼ cups
1kg/2¼lb chicken wings or thighs, skinned
1 onion
2 whole garlic cloves
1 bay leaf
1 sprig of thyme
3–4 sprigs of parsley
10 black peppercorns

1 Cut the chicken into pieces and put into a large, heavy-based saucepan. Peel the onion and stud with the cloves. Tie the bay leaf, thyme, parsley and peppercorns in a piece of muslin and add to the saucepan together with the onion.

2 Pour in 1.75 litres/3 pints/7½ cups cold water. Slowly bring to simmering point, skimming off any scum that rises to the surface with a slotted spoon. Continue to simmer very gently, uncovered, for 1½ hours.

3 Strain the stock through a sieve into a large bowl and leave until cold, then chill. Remove any solidified fat from the surface. Keep chilled in the refrigerator for up to 3–4 days, or freeze in usable amounts.

LOW-FAT MEAT STOCK

─── INGREDIENTS ───

Makes 2 litres/3½ pints/8¾ cups
1.8kg/4lb lean veal bones, trimmed
2 onions, unpeeled, quartered
2 carrots, roughly chopped
2 celery stalks, with leaves if possible, roughly chopped
2 tomatoes, coarsely chopped
a handful of parsley stalks
a few fresh thyme sprigs or 4ml/³⁄₄ tsp dried thyme
2 bay leaves
10 black peppercorns, lightly crushed

1 Put the bones and vegetables in a large stockpot. Add 4.5 litres/7½ pints/4 quarts of water. Bring just to the boil, skimming to remove the foam from the surface. Add the parsley, thyme, bay leaves and peppercorns.

2 Partly cover the pot and simmer the stock for 4–6 hours. The bones and vegetables should always be covered with liquid, so top up with a little boiling water from time to time.

3 Strain the stock through a sieve. Skim as much fat as possible from the surface. If possible, cool the stock and then refrigerate it; the fat will rise to the top and set in a layer that can be removed easily.

VEGETABLE STOCK

─── INGREDIENTS ───

Makes 1.5 litres/2½ pints/6¼ cups
2 carrots
2 celery sticks
2 onions
2 tomatoes
10 mushroom stalks
2 bay leaves
1 sprig of thyme
3–4 sprigs of parsley
10 black peppercorns

1 Roughly chop the vegetables. Place them in a large, heavy-based saucepan. Tie the bay leaves, thyme, parsley and peppercorns in a piece of muslin with some string and add to the pan.

2 Pour in 1.75 litres/3 pints/7½ cups cold water. Slowly bring to simmering point. Continue to simmer very gently, uncovered, for 1½ hours.

3 Strain through a sieve into a large bowl and leave until cold. Keep chilled in the refrigerator for 3–4 days, or freeze in usable amounts.

LOW-FAT SWEET OPTIONS

Desserts needn't be banned from a low-fat, low cholesterol diet. Many traditional dairy products like cream are high in fat, but it's a simple matter to adapt recipes and use low-fat alternatives to create delicious results.

Low-fat yogurt (vanilla is particularly delicious for desserts), fromage frais and reduced-fat crème fraîche may be substituted for cream and skimmed milk can be used in sauces, but here are some further simple ideas to try.

LOW-FAT CREAMY WHIP

A sweetened cream that can be used in place of whipped real dairy cream. It isn't suitable for cooking, but freezes very well.

INGREDIENTS

Makes 150ml/¼ pint/²⁄₃ cup
2.5ml/½ tsp powdered gelatine
50g/2oz/¼ cup skimmed milk powder
15ml/1 tbsp caster sugar
15ml/1 tbsp lemon juice

1 Sprinkle the gelatine over 15ml/ 1 tbsp cold water in a small bowl and leave to 'sponge' for 5 minutes. Place the bowl over a saucepan of hot water and stir until dissolved. Leave to cool.

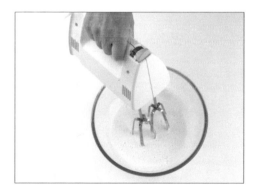

2 Whisk the skimmed milk powder, caster sugar, lemon juice and 60 ml/4 tbsp cold water until frothy. Add the dissolved gelatine and whisk for a few seconds more. Chill in the refrigerator for 30 minutes.

3 Whisk the chilled mixture again until very thick and frothy. Serve within 30 minutes of making.

YOGURT PIPING CREAM

An excellent alternative to whipped cream for decorating cakes and desserts.

INGREDIENTS

Makes 450ml/³⁄₄ pint/scant 2 cups
10ml/2 tsp powdered gelatine
300ml/½ pint/1¼ cups strained yogurt (see right)
15ml/1 tbsp sugar
2.5ml/½ tsp vanilla essence
1 egg white

1 Sprinkle the gelatine over 45ml/ 3 tbsp cold water in a small bowl and leave to 'sponge' for 5 minutes. Place the bowl over a saucepan of hot water and stir until dissolved. Leave to cool.

2 Mix together the yogurt, sugar and vanilla essence. Stir in the gelatine. Chill in the refrigerator for 30 minutes, or until just beginning to set around the edges.

3 Whisk the egg white until stiff and carefully fold it into the yogurt mixture. Spoon into a piping bag fitted with a nozzle and use immediately.

STRAINED YOGURT AND SIMPLE CURD CHEESE

Strained yogurt is simple to make and lower in fat than many commercial varieties. Serve with puddings, instead of cream. Simple curd cheese can be used instead of soured cream, cream cheese or butter, flavoured accordingly for sweet or savoury recipes.

INGREDIENTS

Makes 300ml/½ pint/1¼ cups yogurt or 115g/4oz/½ cup curd cheese
600ml/1 pint/2½ cups natural low-fat yogurt

1 For strained yogurt, line a nylon or stainless-steel sieve with a double layer of muslin. Put over a bowl and pour in the yogurt.

2 Leave to drain in the refrigerator for 3 hours – the mixture will have separated into thick strained yogurt and watery whey. If liked, sweeten with a little honey.

3 To make simple curd cheese, follow step 1 above, then leave to drain in the refrigerator for 8 hours or overnight. Spoon the resulting curd cheese into a bowl, cover and keep chilled until required.

THE FAT AND CALORIE CONTENT OF FOOD
The following figures show the weight of fat (g) and the energy content per 100g/3½ oz of each food.

VEGETABLES

	FAT (g)	SAT. FAT (g)	CHOL (mg)	ENERGY		FAT (g)	SAT. FAT (g)	CHOL (mg)	ENERGY
Broccoli	0.9	0.2	0	33 Kcals/138 kJ	Onions	0.2	trace	0	36 Kcals/151 kJ
Cabbage	0.4	0.1	0	26 Kcals/109 kJ	Peas	1.5	0.3	0	83 Kcals/344 kJ
Carrots	0.3	0.1	0	35 Kcals/146 kJ	Potatoes	0.2	trace	0	75 Kcals/318 kJ
Cauliflower	0.9	0.2	0	34 Kcals/142 kJ	Chips, home-made in dripping	6.7	3.7	6	189 Kcals/796 kJ
Courgettes	0.4	0.1	0	18 Kcals/74 kJ	Chips, retail (in blended oil)	12.4	1.1	0	239 Kcals/1001 kJ
Cucumber	0.1	trace	0	10 Kcals/40 kJ	Oven-chips, frozen, baked	4.2	1.8	0	162 Kcals/687 kJ
Mushrooms	0.5	0.1	0	13 Kcals/55 kJ	Tomatoes	0.3	0.1	0	17 Kcals/73 kJ

BEANS AND PULSES

	FAT (g)	SAT. FAT (g)	CHOL (mg)	ENERGY		FAT (g)	SAT. FAT (g)	CHOL (mg)	ENERGY
Black-eyed beans, cooked	0.7	0.5	0	116 Kcals/494 kJ	Hummus	12.6	n/a	0	187 Kcals/781 kJ
Butter beans, canned	0.5	0.1	0	77 Kcals/327 kJ	Red kidney beans, canned	0.6	0.1	0	100 Kcals/424 kJ
Chick-peas, canned	2.9	0.3	0	115 Kcals/487 kJ	Red lentils, cooked	0.4	trace	0	100 Kcals/424 kJ

FISH AND SEAFOOD

	FAT (g)	SAT. FAT (g)	CHOL (mg)	ENERGY		FAT (g)	SAT. FAT (g)	CHOL (mg)	ENERGY
Cod fillets, raw	0.7	0.1	46	80 Kcals/337 kJ	Prawns, boiled	0.9	0.2	280	99 Kcals/418 kJ
Crab, canned	0.5	0.1	72	77 Kcals/326 kJ	Roe, cod's, fried	11.9	1.2	500	202 Kcals/861 kJ
Haddock, raw	0.6	0.1	36	81 Kcals/345 kJ	Trout, grilled	5.4	1.1	70	135 Kcals/565 kJ
Lemon sole, raw	1.5	0.2	60	83 Kcals/351 kJ	Tuna, canned in brine	0.6	1.4	50	99 Kcals/422 kJ

MEAT AND MEAT PRODUCTS

	FAT (g)	SAT. FAT (g)	CHOL (mg)	ENERGY		FAT (g)	SAT. FAT (g)	CHOL (mg)	ENERGY
Bacon rasher, streaky, raw	23.6	8.2	65	276 Kcals/1142 kJ	Lamb chops, loin, lean and fat	23.0	10.8	79	277 Kcals/1150 kJ
Beef mince, raw	16.2	4.2	56	225 Kcals/934 kJ	Liver, lamb, raw	6.2	1.7	430	137 Kcals/575 kJ
Beef mince, raw, extra lean	9.6	7.1	60	174 Kcals/728 kJ	Pork, average, lean, raw	4.0	1.4	63	123 Kcals/519 kJ
Chicken fillet, raw	1.1	0.3	70	106 Kcals/449 kJ	Pork chops, loin, lean and fat	21.7	8.0	61	270 Kcals/1119 kJ
Chicken, roasted, meat and skin	12.5	3.4	110	218 Kcals/910 kJ	Pork pie	27.0	10.2	52	376 Kcals/1564 kJ
Duck, meat only, raw	6.5	2.0	110	137 Kcals/575 kJ	Rump steak, lean and fat	10.1	4.3	60	174 Kcals/726 kJ
Duck, roasted, meat, fat and skin	38.1	11.4	99	423 Kcals/1750 kJ	Rump steak, lean only	4.1	1.7	59	125 Kcals/526 kJ
					Salami	45.2	n/a	n/a	491 Kcals/2031 kJ
Ham, premium	5.0	1.7	58	132 Kcals/553 kJ	Sausage roll, flaky pastry	36.4	13.4	49	477 Kcals/1985 kJ
Lamb, average, lean, raw	8.3	3.8	74	156 Kcals/651 kJ	Turkey, meat only, raw	1.6	0.5	70	105 Kcals/443 kJ

Information from *The Composition of Foods* (5th edition 1991) is reproduced with the permission of the Royal Society of Chemistry and the Controller of Her Majesty's Stationery Office.

DAIRY, FATS AND OILS

	FAT (g)	SAT. FAT (g)	CHOL (mg)	ENERGY		FAT (g)	SAT. FAT (g)	CHOL (mg)	ENERGY
Brie	26.9	16.8	100	319 Kcals/1323 kJ	Fromage frais, plain	7.1	4.4	25	113 Kcals/469 kJ
Butter	81.7	54	230	737 Kcals/3031kJ	Fromage frais, very low-fat	0.2	0.1	1	58 Kcals/247 kJ
Cream, double	48.0	30	130	449 Kcals/1849 kJ	Greek yogurt	9.1	5.2	n/a	115 Kcals/477 kJ
Cream, single	19.1	11.9	55	198 Kcals/817 kJ	Greek yogurt, reduced-fat	5.0	3.1	13	80 Kcals/335 kJ
Cream, whipping	39.3	24.6	105	373 Kcals/1539 kJ	Lard	99.0	40.8	93	891 Kcals/3663 kJ
Crème fraîche	40.0	25	105	379 Kcals/1567 kJ	Low-fat spread	40.5	11.2	6	390 Kcals/1605 kJ
Crème fraîche, reduced-fat	15.0	9.4	n/a	165 Kcals/683 kJ	Low-fat spread, extra	25	6.5	n/a	273 Kcals/1128 kJ
Cheddar cheese	34.4	21.7	100	412 Kcals/1708 kJ	Low-fat yogurt, plain	0.8	0.5	4	56 Kcals/236 kJ
Cheddar-type, reduced-fat	15.0	9.4	43	261 Kcals/1091 kJ	Margarine, polyunsaturated	81.6	16.2	7	739 Kcals/3039 kJ
Corn oil	99.9	12.7	0	899 Kcals/3696 kJ	Mayonnaise	75.6	11.1	75	691 Kcals/2843 kJ
Cream cheese	47.4	29.7	95	439 Kcals/1807 kJ	Mayonnaise, reduced calorie	28.1	4.5	n/a	288 Kcals/1188 kJ
Edam cheese	25.4	15.9	80	333 Kcals/1382 kJ	Milk, semi-skimmed	1.6	1.0	7	46 Kcals/195 kJ
Egg, whole	10.8	3.1	385	147 Kcals/612 kJ	Milk, skimmed	0.1	0.1	2	33 Kcals/130 kJ
Egg white	trace	trace	trace	36 Kcals/153 kJ	Milk, whole	3.9	2.4	14	66 Kcals/275 kJ
Egg yolk	30.5	8.7	1120	339 Kcals/1402 kJ	Olive oil	99.9	14	0	899 Kcals/3696 kJ
Fat-free dressing	1.2	0	0	67 Kcals/282 kJ	Parmesan cheese	32.7	20.5	100	452 Kcals/1880 kJ
Feta cheese	20.2	13.7	70	250 Kcals/1037 kJ	Safflower oil	99.9	10.2	0	899 Kcals/3696 kJ
French dressing	49.4	10	0	462 Kcals/1902 kJ	Skimmed milk soft cheese	trace	trace	1	74 Kcals/313 kJ

CEREALS, BAKING AND PRESERVES

	FAT (g)	SAT. FAT (g)	CHOL (mg)	ENERGY		FAT (g)	SAT. FAT (g)	CHOL (mg)	ENERGY
Bread, brown	2.0	0.4	0	218 Kcals/927 kJ	Honey	0	0	0	288 Kcals/1229 kJ
Bread, white	1.9	0.4	0	235 Kcals/1002 kJ	Lemon curd, home-made	0.8	0.3	150	176 Kcals/736 kJ
Bread, wholemeal	2.5	0.5	0	215 Kcals/914 kJ	Madeira cake	16.9	17.3	n/a	393 Kcals/1652 kJ
Chocolate, milk	30.3	17.8	30	520 Kcals/2214 kJ	Pasta, white, uncooked	1.8	0.2	0	342 Kcals/1456 kJ
Chocolate, plain	29.2	16.9	0	510 Kcals/2157 kJ	Pasta, wholemeal, uncooked	2.5	0.4	0	324 Kcals/1379 kJ
Cornflakes	0.7	0.1	0	360 Kcals/1535 kJ	Rice, brown, uncooked	2.8	0.7	0	357 Kcals/1518 kJ
Croissant	20.3	6.5	75	360 Kcals/1505 kJ	Rice, white, uncooked	3.6	0.9	0	383 Kcals/1630 kJ
Digestive biscuit, plain	20.9	8.6	41	471 Kcals/1978 kJ	Shortbread	26.1	17.3	74	498 Kcals/2087 kJ
Doughnut, jam	14.5	4.3	15	336 Kcals/1414 kJ	Sponge cake, fatless	6.1	1.7	223	294 Kcals/1245 kJ
Flapjack	26.6	7.6	43	484 Kcals/2028 kJ	Sugar, white	0	0	0	105 Kcals/394 kJ
Fruit cake, rich	11	3.4	63	341 Kcals/1438 kJ	Sultana bran	1.6	0.4	0	303 Kcals/1289 kJ
Fruit jam	0	0	0	261 Kcals/1116 kJ	Swiss-style muesli	5.9	0.8	trace	363 Kcals/1540 kJ

FRUIT AND NUTS

	FAT (g)	SAT. FAT (g)	CHOL (mg)	ENERGY		FAT (g)	SAT. FAT (g)	CHOL (mg)	ENERGY
Almonds	55.8	4.7	0	612 Kcals/2534 kJ	Hazelnuts	63.5	4.7	0	650 Kcals/2685 kJ
Apples, eating	0.1	trace	0	47 Kcals/199 kJ	Oranges	0.1	trace	0	37 Kcals/158 kJ
Avocados	19.5	4.1	0	190 Kcals/784 kJ	Peaches	0.1	trace	0	33 Kcals/142 kJ
Bananas	0.3	0.1	0	95 Kcals/403 kJ	Peanut butter, smooth	53.7	11.7	0	623 Kcals/2581 kJ
Brazil nuts	68.2	16.4	0	682 Kcals/2813 kJ	Pears	0.1	trace	0	40 Kcals/169 kJ
Dried mixed fruit	0.4	n/a	0	268 Kcals/1114 kJ	Pine nuts	68.6	4.6	0	688 Kcals/2840 kJ
Grapefruit	0.1	trace	0	30 Kcals/126 kJ	Walnuts	68.5	5.6	0	688 Kcals/2837kJ

SOUPS AND STARTERS

For a healthy diet it makes good sense to include some home-made soups in everyday meals, packed with the goodness of fresh ingredients and very low in fat. As a light lunch with crusty wholemeal bread, or as a starter, modern soups are extremely quick and easy to make. An added bonus is the wonderful variety of fresh, seasonal vegetables available all year so that soups, such as Mushroom, Celery and Garlic Soup and Red Pepper Soup with Lime, can be enjoyed all year round. Other starters can double up as a light meal or snack; such as Lemony Stuffed Courgettes and Cucumber and Alfalfa Tortillas.

CAULIFLOWER AND WALNUT CREAM

Even though there's no cream added to this soup, the cauliflower gives it a delicious, rich, creamy texture.

INGREDIENTS

Serves 4

1 medium cauliflower
1 medium onion, roughly chopped
450ml/¾ pint/1⅞ cups chicken or
 vegetable stock
450ml/¾ pint/1⅞ cups skimmed milk
45ml/3 tbsp walnut pieces
salt and black pepper
paprika and chopped walnuts, to
 garnish

1 Trim the cauliflower of outer leaves and break into small florets. Place the cauliflower, onion and stock in a large saucepan.

2 Bring to the boil, cover and simmer for about 15 minutes, or until soft. Add the milk and walnuts, then purée in a food processor until smooth.

3 Season the soup to taste, then bring to the boil. Serve sprinkled with paprika and chopped walnuts.

NUTRITION NOTES

Per portion:

Energy	166Kcals/699kJ
Fat	9.02g
Saturated fat	0.88g
Cholesterol	2.25mg
Fibre	2.73g

CURRIED CARROT AND APPLE SOUP

INGREDIENTS

Serves 4

10ml/2 tsp sunflower oil
15ml/1 tbsp mild Korma curry powder
500g/1¼ lb carrots, chopped
1 large onion, chopped
1 Bramley cooking apple, chopped
750ml/1¼ pints/3⅔ cups chicken stock
salt and black pepper
natural low fat yogurt and carrot curls,
 to garnish

NUTRITION NOTES

Per portion:

Energy	114Kcals/477kJ
Fat	3.57g
Saturated fat	0.43g
Cholesterol	0.4mg
Fibre	4.99g

1 Heat the oil and gently fry the curry powder for 2–3 minutes.

2 Add the carrots, onion and apple, stir well, then cover the pan.

3 Cook over a very low heat for about 15 minutes, shaking the pan occasionally until softened. Spoon the vegetable mixture into a food processor or blender, then add half the stock and process until smooth.

4 Return to the pan and pour in the remaining stock. Bring the soup to the boil and adjust the seasoning before serving in bowls, garnished with a swirl of yogurt and a few curls of carrot.

TOMATO AND CORIANDER SOUP

This delicious soup is an ideal solution when time is short but you still want to produce a very stylish starter.

INGREDIENTS

Serves 4

675g/1½lb small fresh tomatoes
30ml/2 tbsp vegetable oil
1 bay leaf
4 spring onions, cut into 2.5cm/1in
  pieces
5ml/1 tsp salt
5ml/1 tsp garlic pulp
5ml/1 tsp crushed black
  peppercorns
30ml/2 tbsp chopped fresh
  coriander
750ml/1¼ pints/3 cups water
15ml/1 tbsp cornflour
60ml/4 tbsp single cream, to garnish

1 To skin the tomatoes, plunge them into very hot water for 30 seconds, then transfer to a bowl of cold water. The skin should now peel off quickly and easily. Chop the tomatoes into large chunks.

2 Heat the oil in a large saucepan, add the bay leaf and spring onions, then stir in the tomatoes. Cook, stirring, for a few minutes more until the tomatoes are softened.

3 Add the salt, garlic, peppercorns, coriander and water, bring to the boil, then simmer for 15 minutes.

4 Dissolve the cornflour in a little water. Remove the soup from the heat and press through a sieve.

5 Return the soup to the pan, add the cornflour mixture and stir over a gentle heat until boiling and thickened.

6 Ladle the soup into shallow soup plates, then swirl a tablespoon of cream into each bowl before serving.

NUTRITION NOTES

Per portion:

Energy	129Kcals/474kJ
Fat	9.0g
Saturated fat	2.51g
Cholesterol	8.3mg
Fibre	1.9g

RED PEPPER SOUP WITH LIME

The beautiful rich red colour of this soup makes it a very attractive starter or light lunch. For a special dinner, toast some tiny croutons and serve sprinkled into the soup.

INGREDIENTS

Serves 4–6
4 red peppers, seeded and chopped
1 large onion, chopped
5ml/1 tsp olive oil
1 garlic clove, crushed
1 small red chilli, sliced
45ml/3 tbsp tomato purée
900ml/1½ pints/3¾ cups chicken stock
finely grated rind and juice of 1 lime
salt and black pepper
shreds of lime rind, to garnish

1 Cook the onion and peppers gently in the oil in a covered saucepan for about 5 minutes, shaking the pan occasionally, until softened.

2 Stir in the garlic, then add the chilli with the tomato purée. Stir in half the stock, then bring to the boil. Cover the pan and simmer for 10 minutes.

3 Cool slightly, then purée in a food processor or blender. Return to the pan, then add the remaining stock, the lime rind and juice, and seasoning.

4 Bring the soup back to the boil, then serve at once with a few strips of lime rind, scattered into each bowl.

NUTRITION NOTES	
Per portion:	
Energy	87Kcals/366kJ
Fat	1.57g
Saturated fat	0.12g
Cholesterol	0
Fibre	3.40g

MEDITERRANEAN TOMATO SOUP

Children will love this soup – especially if you use fancy shapes of pasta such as alphabet or animal shapes.

INGREDIENTS

Serves 4

675g/1½ lb ripe plum tomatoes
1 medium onion, quartered
1 celery stick
1 garlic clove
15ml/1 tbsp olive oil
450ml/¾ pint/1⅞ cups chicken stock
15ml/2 tbsp tomato purée
50g/2oz/½ cup small pasta shapes
salt and black pepper
fresh coriander or parsley, to garnish

1 Place the tomatoes, onion, celery and garlic in a pan with the oil. Cover and cook over a low heat for 40–45 minutes, shaking the pan occasionally, until very soft.

2 Spoon the vegetables into a food processor or blender and process until smooth. Press though a sieve, then return to the pan.

3 Stir in the stock and tomato purée and bring to the boil. Add the pasta and simmer gently for about 8 minutes, or until the pasta is tender. Add salt and pepper, to taste, then sprinkle with coriander or parsley and serve hot.

NUTRITION NOTES

Per portion:

Energy	112Kcals/474kJ
Fat	3.61g
Saturated fat	0.49g
Cholesterol	0
Fibre	2.68g

MUSHROOM, CELERY AND GARLIC SOUP

INGREDIENTS

Serves 4

350g/12oz/3 cups chopped mushrooms
4 celery sticks, chopped
3 garlic cloves
45ml/3 tbsp dry sherry or white wine
750ml/1¼ pints/3⅔cups chicken stock
30ml/2 tbsp Worcestershire sauce
5ml/1 tsp grated nutmeg
salt and black pepper
celery leaves, to garnish

NUTRITION NOTES

Per portion:

Energy	48Kcals/200kJ
Fat	1.09g
Saturated fat	0.11g
Cholesterol	0
Fibre	1.64g

1 Place the mushrooms, celery and garlic in a pan and stir in the sherry or wine. Cover and cook over a low heat for 30–40 minutes, until tender.

2 Add half the stock and purée in a food processor or blender until smooth. Return to the pan and add the remaining stock, the Worcestershire sauce and nutmeg.

3 Bring to the boil, season and serve hot, garnished with celery leaves.

MUSHROOM CROUSTADES

The rich mushroom flavour of this filling is heightened by the addition of Worcestershire sauce.

Serves 2–4

1 short French stick, about 25cm/10in
10ml/2 tsp olive oil
250g/9oz open cup mushrooms, quartered
10ml/2 tsp Worcestershire sauce
10ml/2 tsp lemon juice
30ml/2 tbsp skimmed milk
30ml/2 tbsp snipped fresh chives
salt and black pepper
snipped fresh chives, to garnish

1 Preheat the oven to 200°C/400°F/Gas 6. Cut the French bread in half lengthways. Cut a scoop out of the soft middle of each, leaving a thick border all the way round.

2 Brush the bread with oil, place on a baking sheet and bake for about 6–8 minutes, until golden and crisp.

3 Place the mushrooms in a small saucepan with the Worcestershire sauce, lemon juice and milk. Simmer for about 5 minutes, or until most of the liquid is evaporated.

4 Remove from the heat, then add the chives and seasoning. Spoon into the bread croustades and serve hot, garnished with snipped chives.

NUTRITION NOTES	
Per portion:	
Energy	324Kcals/1361kJ
Fat	6.4g
Saturated fat	1.27g
Cholesterol	0.3mg
Fibre	3.07g

CUCUMBER AND ALFALFA TORTILLAS

Wheat tortillas are extremely simple to prepare at home. Served with a crisp, fresh salsa, they make a marvellous starter, light lunch or supper dish.

INGREDIENTS

Serves 4
225g/8oz/2 cups plain flour, sifted
pinch of salt
45ml/3 tbsp olive oil
100–150ml/4–5fl oz/½–⅔ cup warm
    water
lime wedges, to garnish

For the salsa
1 red onion, finely chopped
1 red chilli, seeded and finely chopped
30ml/2 tbsp chopped fresh dill or
    coriander
½ cucumber, peeled and chopped
175g/6oz/2 cups alfalfa sprouts

For the sauce
1 large ripe avocado, peeled and stoned
juice of 1 lime
15ml/2 tbsp soft goat's cheese
pinch of paprika

1 Mix all the salsa ingredients together in a bowl and set aside.

2 For the sauce, place the avocado, lime juice and goat's cheese in a food processor or blender and process until smooth. Place in a bowl and cover with clear film. Dust with paprika just before serving.

3 For the tortillas, place the flour and salt in a food processor or blender, add the oil and process. Gradually add the water until a stiff dough has formed. Turn out on to a floured board and knead until smooth.

4 Divide the mixture into eight pieces. Knead each piece for a couple of minutes and form into a ball. Flatten and roll out each ball to a 23cm/9 in circle.

NUTRITION NOTES	
Per portion:	
Energy	395Kcals/1659kJ
Fat	20.17g
Saturated fat	1.69g
Cholesterol	4.38mg
Fibre	4.15g

5 Heat a non-stick or ungreased heavy-based pan. Cook one tortilla at a time for about 30 seconds on each side. Place the cooked tortillas in a clean dish towel and repeat until you have made eight tortillas.

6 Spread each tortilla with a spoonful of avocado sauce, top with the salsa and roll up. Serve garnished with lime wedges and eat immediately.

COOK'S TIP
When peeling the avocado be sure to scrape off the bright green flesh from immediately under the skin as this gives the sauce its vivid green colour.

CHEESE AND SPINACH PUFFS

INGREDIENTS

Serves 6

150g/5oz cooked, chopped spinach
175g/6oz/¾ cup cottage cheese
5ml/1 tsp grated nutmeg
2 egg whites
30ml/2 tbsp grated Parmesan cheese
salt and black pepper

1 Preheat the oven to 220°C/425°F/ Gas 7. Oil six ramekin dishes.

2 Mix together the spinach and cottage cheese in a small bowl, then add the nutmeg and seasoning to taste.

3 Whisk the egg whites in a separate bowl until stiff enough to hold soft peaks. Fold them evenly into the spinach mixture using a spatula or large metal spoon, then spoon the mixture into the oiled ramekins, dividing it evenly, and smooth the tops.

4 Sprinkle with the Parmesan and place on a baking sheet. Bake for 15–20 minutes, or until well risen and golden brown. Serve immediately.

NUTRITION NOTES	
Per portion:	
Energy	47Kcals/195kJ
Fat	1.32g
Saturated fat	0.52g
Cholesterol	2.79mg
Fibre	0.53g

LEMONY STUFFED COURGETTES

INGREDIENTS

Serves 4

4 courgettes, about 175g/6oz each
5ml/1 tsp sunflower oil
1 garlic clove, crushed
5ml/1 tsp ground lemon grass
finely grated rind and juice of ½ lemon
115g/4oz/1½ cups cooked long grain
   rice
175g/6oz cherry tomatoes, halved
30ml/2 tbsp toasted cashew nuts
salt and black pepper
sprigs of thyme, to garnish

NUTRITION NOTES	
Per portion:	
Energy	126Kcals/530kJ
Fat	5.33g
Saturated fat	0.65g
Cholesterol	0
Fibre	2.31g

1 Preheat the oven to 200°C/400°F/ Gas 6. Halve the courgettes lengthways and use a teaspoon to scoop out the centres. Blanch the shells in boiling water for 1 minute, then drain well.

2 Chop the courgette flesh finely and place in a saucepan with the oil and garlic. Stir over a moderate heat until softened, but not browned.

3 Stir in the lemon grass, lemon rind and juice, rice, tomatoes and cashew nuts. Season well and spoon into the courgette shells. Place the shells in a baking tin and cover with foil.

4 Bake for 25–30 minutes or until the courgettes are tender, then serve hot, garnished with thyme sprigs.

PASTA, PIZZAS, PULSES AND GRAINS

Pasta, pizzas, pulses and grain dishes should be encouraged at family meals as they're very healthy foods. They contain good amounts of protein, carbohydrates and vitamins, and are versatile and usually low in fat. The recipes in this section provide lots of ideas for using these ingredients in tasty and exciting new ways. Add variety to meals by introducing different grains, such as polenta and couscous — they are just as healthy as rice and pasta, and just as delicious — try Baked Polenta with Tomatoes and Sweet Vegetable Couscous.

SPINACH AND HAZELNUT LASAGNE

A vegetarian dish which is hearty enough to satisfy meat-eaters too. Use frozen spinach if you're short of time.

INGREDIENTS

Serves 4
900g/2 lb fresh spinach
300ml/½ pint/1¼ cups vegetable or
    chicken stock
1 medium onion, finely chopped
1 garlic clove, crushed
75g/3oz/¾ cup hazelnuts
30ml/2 tbsp chopped fresh basil
6 sheets lasagne
400g/14oz can chopped tomatoes
200g/7oz/1 cup low fat fromage frais
flaked hazelnuts and chopped parsley,
    to garnish

1 Preheat the oven to 200°C/400°F/ Gas 6. Wash the spinach and place in a pan with just the water that clings to the leaves. Cook the spinach on a fairly high heat for 2 minutes until wilted. Drain well.

2 Heat 30ml/2 tbsp of the stock in a large pan and simmer the onion and garlic until soft. Stir in the spinach, hazelnuts and basil.

3 In a large ovenproof dish, layer the spinach, lasagne and tomatoes. Season well between the layers. Pour over the remaining stock. Spread the fromage frais over the top.

4 Bake the lasagne for about 45 minutes, or until golden brown. Serve hot, sprinkled with lines of flaked hazelnuts and chopped parsley.

COOK'S TIP
The flavour of hazelnuts is improved by roasting. Place them on a baking sheet and bake in a moderate oven, or under a hot grill, until light golden.

NUTRITION NOTES

Per portion:
Energy	365Kcals/1532kJ
Fat	17g
Saturated fat	1.46g
Cholesterol	0.5mg
Fibre	8.16g

TAGLIATELLE WITH PEA AND BEAN SAUCE

A creamy pea sauce makes a wonderful combination with the crunchy young vegetables.

INGREDIENTS

Serves 4

15ml/1 tbsp olive oil
1 garlic clove, crushed
6 spring onions, sliced
115g/4oz/1 cup fresh or frozen baby
   peas, defrosted
350g/12oz fresh young asparagus
30ml/2 tbsp chopped fresh sage, plus
   extra leaves, to garnish
finely grated rind of 2 lemons
400ml/14fl oz/1⅔ cups vegetable stock
   or water
225g/8oz/1½ cups fresh or frozen
   broad beans, defrosted
450g/1 lb tagliatelle
60ml/4 tbsp low fat natural yogurt

NUTRITION NOTES

Per portion:	
Energy	509 Kcals/2139kJ
Fat	6.75g
Saturated fat	0.95g
Cholesterol	0.6mg
Fibre	9.75g

1 Heat the oil in a pan. Add the garlic and spring onions, and cook gently for about 2–3 minutes until softened.

2 Add the peas and a third of the asparagus, together with the sage, lemon rind and stock or water. Simmer for about 10 minutes. Process in a food processor or blender until smooth.

3 Meanwhile remove the outer skins from the broad beans and discard.

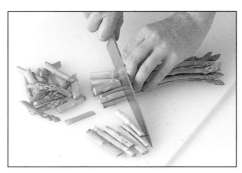

4 Cut the remaining asparagus into 5cm/2 in lengths, trimming off any tough fibrous stems, and blanch in boiling water for about 2 minutes.

5 Cook the tagliatelle following the manufacturer's instructions until *al dente*. Drain well.

6 Add the cooked asparagus and shelled beans to the sauce, and reheat. Stir in the yogurt and toss into the tagliatelle. Garnish with a few extra sage leaves, and serve immediately.

COOK'S TIP
Frozen peas and beans have been suggested as an option here to cut down the preparation time, but the dish tastes even better if you use fresh young vegetables when in season.

PASTA WITH PASSATA AND CHICK PEAS

INGREDIENTS

Serves 4

300g/10oz/2 cups pasta
5ml/1 tsp olive oil
1 small onion, finely chopped
1 garlic clove, crushed
1 celery stick, finely chopped
425g/15oz can chick-peas, drained
250ml/8 fl oz/1 cup passata
salt and black pepper
chopped fresh parsley, to garnish

1 Heat the olive oil in a non-stick pan and fry the onion, garlic and celery until softened but not browned. Stir in the chick-peas and passata, then cover and simmer for about 15 minutes.

2 Cook the pasta in a large pan of boiling, lightly salted water until just tender. Drain the pasta and toss into the sauce, then season to taste with salt and pepper. Sprinkle with chopped fresh parsley, then serve hot.

NUTRITION NOTES

Per portion:

Energy	374Kcals/1570kJ
Fat	4.44g
Saturated fat	0.32g
Cholesterol	0
Fibre	6.41g

PEPERONATA PIZZA

INGREDIENTS

Makes 2 large pizzas

450g/1 lb/4 cups plain flour
pinch of salt
1 sachet easy-blend yeast
about 350ml/12 fl oz/1½ cups warm
    water

For the topping

1 onion, sliced
10ml/2 tsp olive oil
2 large red and 2 yellow peppers,
    seeded and sliced
1 garlic clove, crushed
400g/14oz can tomatoes
8 pitted black olives, halved
salt and black pepper

NUTRITION NOTES

Per portion:

Energy	965Kcals/4052kJ
Fat	9.04g
Saturated fat	1.07g
Cholesterol	0
Fibre	14.51g

1 To make the dough, sift the flour and salt into a bowl and stir in the yeast. Stir in just enough warm water to mix to a soft dough.

2 Knead for 5 minutes until smooth. Cover and leave in a warm place for about 1 hour, or until doubled in size.

3 To make the topping, fry the onion in the oil until soft, then stir in the peppers, garlic and tomatoes. Cover and simmer for 30 minutes, until no free liquid remains. Season to taste.

4 Preheat the oven to 230°C /450°F/ Gas 8. Divide the dough in half and press out each piece on a lightly oiled baking sheet to a 28cm/11in round, turning up the edges slightly.

5 Spread over the topping, dot with olives and bake for 15–20 minutes. Serve hot or cold with salad.

TABBOULEH WITH FENNEL

A fresh salad originating in the Middle East that is perfect for a summer lunch. Serve with lettuce and pitta bread.

INGREDIENTS

Serves 4

225g/8oz/1¼ cups bulgur wheat
2 fennel bulbs
1 small red chilli, seeded and chopped
1 celery stick, finely sliced
30ml/2 tbsp olive oil
finely grated rind and juice of
   2 lemons
6–8 spring onions, chopped
90ml/6 tbsp chopped fresh mint
90ml/6 tbsp chopped fresh parsley
1 pomegranate, seeded
salt and black pepper

NUTRITION NOTES

Per portion:
Energy	188Kcals/791kJ
Fat	4.67g
Saturated fat	0.62g
Cholesterol	0
Fibre	2.17g

1 Place the bulgur wheat in a bowl and pour over enough cold water to cover. Leave to stand for 30 minutes.

3 Halve the fennel bulbs and carefully cut into very fine slices with a sharp knife.

2 Drain the wheat through a sieve, pressing out any excess water using a spoon.

4 Mix all the remaining ingredients together, including the soaked bulgur wheat and fennel. Season well, cover, and set aside for 30 minutes before serving.

COOK'S TIP
Fennel has a very distinctive aniseed flavour. When you are buying fennel, choose well-rounded bulbs which are pale green to white in colour. Avoid any that are deep green. Fennel never goes out of season, it is available all year round.

SWEET VEGETABLE COUSCOUS

A wonderful combination of sweet vegetables and spices, this makes a substantial winter dish.

INGREDIENTS

Serves 4–6

generous pinch of saffron threads
45ml/3 tbsp boiling water
15ml/1 tbsp olive oil
1 red onion, sliced
2 garlic cloves
1–2 red chillies, seeded and finely chopped
2.5ml/½ tsp ground ginger
2.5ml/½ tsp ground cinnamon
400g/14oz can chopped tomatoes
300ml/½ pint/1¼ cups fresh vegetable stock or water
4 carrots, peeled and cut into 5mm/¼ in slices
2 turnips, peeled and cut into 2cm/¼ in cubes
450g/1 lb sweet potatoes, peeled and cut into 2cm/¼ in cubes
75g/3oz/½ cup raisins
2 courgettes, cut into 5mm/¼ in slices
400g/14oz can chick-peas, drained and rinsed
45ml/3 tbsp chopped fresh parsley
45ml/3 tbsp chopped fresh coriander
450g/1 lb/4 cups quick-cook couscous

1 Leave the saffron to infuse in the boiling water.

2 Heat the oil in a large saucepan or flameproof casserole. Add the onion, garlic and chillies, and cook gently for about 5 minutes.

3 Add the ground ginger and cinnamon, and gently cook for a further 1–2 minutes.

4 Add the tomatoes, stock or water, saffron and liquid, carrots, turnips, sweet potatoes and raisins, cover and simmer for a further 25 minutes.

5 Add the courgettes, chick-peas, parsley and coriander, and cook for a further 10 minutes.

6 Meanwhile prepare the couscous following the manufacturer's instructions, and then serve with the prepared vegetables.

NUTRITION NOTES

Per portion:

Energy	570Kcals/2393kJ
Fat	7.02g
Saturated fat	0.83g
Cholesterol	0
Fibre	10.04g

COOK'S TIP

Vegetable stock can be made from a variety of uncooked vegetables. These can include the outer leaves of cabbage, lettuce and other greens, carrot peelings, leeks and parsnips.

THAI FRAGRANT RICE

A lovely, soft, fluffy rice dish, perfumed with delicious and fresh lemon grass.

INGREDIENTS

Serves 4

1 piece lemon grass
2 limes
225g/8oz/1⅓ cups brown basmati rice
15ml/1 tbsp olive oil
1 onion, chopped
2.5cm/1 in piece fresh root ginger, peeled and finely chopped
7.5ml/1½ tsp coriander seeds
7.5ml/1½ tsp cumin seeds
750ml/1¼ pints/3⅔ cups vegetable stock
60ml/4 tbsp chopped fresh coriander
lime wedges, to serve

> COOK'S TIP
> Other varieties of rice, such as white basmati or long grain, can be used for this dish but you will need to adjust the cooking times as necessary.

1 Finely chop the lemon grass and remove the zest from the limes.

2 Rinse the rice in cold water. Drain through a sieve.

3 Heat the oil in a large saucepan and add the onion and spices and cook gently for about 2–3 minutes.

4 Add the rice and cook for a further minute, then add the stock or water and bring to the boil. Reduce the heat to very low and cover the pan. Cook gently for about 30 minutes then check the rice. If it is still crunchy, cover the pan again with the lid and leave for a further 3–5 minutes. Remove from the heat.

5 Stir in the fresh coriander, fluff up the grains, cover and leave for 10 minutes. Serve with lime wedges.

NUTRITION NOTES	
Per portion:	
Energy	259Kcals/1087kJ
Fat	5.27g
Saturated fat	0.81g
Cholesterol	0
Fibre	1.49g

PUMPKIN AND PISTACHIO RISOTTO

This elegant combination of creamy golden rice and orange pumpkin can be made as pale or bright as you like – simply add different quantities of saffron.

INGREDIENTS

Serves 4

1.2 litres/2 pints/5 cups vegetable stock
or water
generous pinch of saffron threads
30ml/2 tbsp olive oil
1 onion, chopped
2 garlic cloves, crushed
900g/2 lb pumpkin, peeled, seeded and
cut into 2cm/³/₄ in cubes
450g/1 lb/2 cups arborio rice
200ml/7fl oz/⅞ cup dry white wine
15ml/1 tbsp Parmesan cheese, finely
grated
50g/2oz/½cup pistachios
45ml/3 tbsp chopped fresh marjoram
or oregano, plus extra leaves, to
garnish
salt, freshly grated nutmeg and black
pepper

NUTRITION NOTES

Per portion:
Energy	630Kcals/2646kJ
Fat	15.24g
Saturated fat	2.66g
Cholesterol	3.75mg
Fibre	2.59g

1 Bring the stock or water to the boil and reduce to a low simmer. Ladle a little liquid into a small bowl. Add the saffron threads and leave to infuse.

2 Heat the oil in a saucepan or flame-proof casserole. Add the onion and garlic, and cook gently for 5 minutes until softened. Add the pumpkin and rice and cook for a few more minutes until the rice looks transparent.

3 Pour in the wine and allow it to boil hard. When it is absorbed add a quarter of the stock or water and the infused saffron and liquid. Stir constantly until all the liquid is absorbed.

4 Gradually add a ladleful of stock or water at a time, allowing the rice to absorb the liquid before adding more and stir constantly.

5 Cook the rice for about 25–30 minutes or until *al dente*. Stir in the Parmesan cheese, cover the pan and leave to stand for 5 minutes.

6 To finish, stir in the pistachios and marjoram or oregano. Season to taste with a little salt, nutmeg and pepper, and sprinkle over a few extra marjoram or oregano leaves.

COOK'S TIP
Italian arborio rice is a special short grain rice that gives an authentic creamy consistency.

CORN GRIDDLE PANCAKES

These crisp pancakes are delicious to serve as a snack lunch, or as a light supper with a crisp mixed salad.

INGREDIENTS

Serves 4, makes about 12
115g/4oz/1 cup self-raising flour
1 egg white
150ml/¼ pint/⅔ cup skimmed milk
200g/7oz can sweetcorn, drained
oil, for brushing
salt and black pepper
tomato chutney, to serve

1 Place the flour, egg white and skimmed milk in a food processor or blender with half the sweetcorn and process until smooth.

2 Season the batter well and add the remaining sweetcorn.

3 Heat a frying pan and brush with oil. Drop in tablespoons of batter and cook until set. Turn over the pancakes and cook the other side until golden. Serve hot with tomato chutney.

NUTRITION NOTES

Per portion:
Energy	162Kcals/680kJ
Fat	0.89g
Saturated fat	0.14g
Cholesterol	0.75mg
Fibre	1.49g

BAKED POLENTA WITH TOMATOES

INGREDIENTS

Serves 4
750ml/1¼ pints/3⅔ cups stock
175g/6oz/1⅛ cup polenta (coarse corn-meal)
60ml/4 tbsp chopped fresh sage
5ml/1 tsp olive oil
2 beefsteak tomatoes, sliced
15ml/1 tbsp grated Parmesan cheese
salt and black pepper

1 Bring the stock to the boil in a large saucepan, then gradually stir in the polenta.

2 Continue stirring the polenta over a moderate heat for about 5 minutes, until the mixture begins to come away from the sides of the pan. Stir in the chopped sage and season well, then spoon into a lightly oiled, shallow 23 x 33cm/9x13 in tin and spread evenly. Leave to cool.

3 Preheat the oven to 200°C/400°F/ Gas 6. Cut the cooled polenta into 24 squares using a sharp knife.

4 Arrange the polenta overlapping with tomato slices in a lightly oiled, shallow ovenproof dish. Sprinkle with Parmesan and bake for 20 minutes or until golden brown. Serve hot.

NUTRITION NOTES

Per portion:
Energy	200Kcals/842kJ
Fat	3.8g
Saturated fat	0.77g
Cholesterol	1.88mg
Fibre	1.71g

MEAT AND POULTRY

There's no reason why meat should not be a valuable part of a low-fat, low cholesterol diet, but you need to make careful choices when shopping and adapt preparation and cooking methods to keep fats to a minimum. Poultry is an obvious choice for a low-fat diet; endlessly versatile and economical, it is mostly very low in fat, and much of the fat it does contain is low in saturates. Tempt your family with dishes such as Sausage and Beans with Dumplings, Turkey and Macaroni Cheese and Barbecued Chicken. You'll soon discover that meat and poultry have a full part to play in a low-fat, low cholesterol diet.

THAI BEEF SALAD

A hearty salad of beef, laced with a chilli and lime dressing.

INGREDIENTS

Serves 6
75g/3oz lean sirloin steaks
1 red onion, finely sliced
1/2 cucumber, finely sliced
   into matchsticks
1 lemon grass stalk, finely chopped
30ml/2 tbsp chopped spring onions
juice of 2 limes
15–30ml/1–2 tbsp fish sauce
2–4 red chillies, finely sliced, to garnish
fresh coriander, Chinese mustard cress
   and mint leaves, to garnish

NUTRITION NOTES

Per portion:
Energy	101Kcals/424kJ
Fat	3.8g
Saturated fat	1.7g
Cholesterol	33.4mg
Fibre	0.28g

COOK'S TIP
Rump or fillet steaks would work just as well in this recipe. Choose good-quality lean steaks and remove and discard any visible fat.

1 Grill the sirloin steaks until they are medium-rare, then allow to rest for 10–15 minutes.

2 When cool, thinly slice the beef and put the slices in a large bowl.

3 Add the sliced onion, cucumber matchsticks and lemon grass.

4 Add the spring onions. Toss and season with lime juice and fish sauce. Serve at room temperature or chilled, garnished with the chillies, coriander, mustard cress and mint.

SPICED LAMB WITH VEGETABLE COUSCOUS

A delicious stew of lamb and
vegetables served with couscous.

INGREDIENTS

Serves 6

350g/12oz lean lamb fillet, cut into
2 cm/³⁄₄ in cubes
30ml/2 tbsp wholemeal plain flour,
10ml/2 tsp sunflower oil
1 onion, chopped
2 garlic cloves, crushed
1 red pepper, seeded and diced
5ml/1 tsp ground coriander
5ml/1 tsp ground cumin
5ml/1 tsp ground allspice
2.5ml/¹⁄₂ tsp hot chilli powder
300ml/¹⁄₂ pint/1¹⁄₄ cups lamb stock
400g/14oz can choppped tomatoes
225g/8oz carrots, sliced
175g/6oz parsnips, sliced
175g/6oz courgettes, sliced
175g/6oz mushrooms, quartered
225g/8oz frozen broad beans
115g/4oz/²⁄₃ cup sultanas
450g/1 lb quick-cook couscous
salt and ground black pepper
fresh coriander, to garnish

1 Toss the lamb in the flour. Heat the
oil in a large saucepan and add the
lamb, onion, garlic and pepper. Cook
for 5 minutes, stirring frequently.

NUTRITION NOTES

Per portion:

Energy	439Kcals/1844kJ
Fat	8.6g
Saturated fat	2.88g
Cholesterol	49.6mg
Fibre	7.2g

2 Add any remaining flour and the
spices and cook for 1 minute,
stirring.

3 Gradually add the stock, stirring
continuously, then add the
tomatoes, carrots and parsnips and
mix well. Bring to the boil, stirring
then cover and simmer for 30 minutes,
stirring occasionally.

4 Add the courgettes, mushrooms,
broad beans and sultanas. Cover,
return to the boil and simmer for a
further 20–30 minutes, until the lamb
and vegetables are tender, stirring
occasionally. Season to taste.

5 Meanwhile, soak the couscous and
steam in a lined colander over a pan
of boiling water for about 20 minutes,
until cooked, or according to the
packet instructions. Pile the couscous
on to a warmed serving platter or
individual plates and top with the lamb
and vegetable stew. Garnish with fresh
coriander and serve immediately.

BEEF AND LENTIL PIES

In this variation of cottage pie, lentils are substituted for some of the meat to produce a dish that is lower in fat and higher in fibre. Some red meat is included to boost the iron content.

INGREDIENTS

Serves 4

175g/6oz/1 cup green lentils
225g/8oz extra lean minced beef
1 onion, chopped
2 celery sticks, chopped
1 large carrot, chopped
1 garlic clove, crushed
425g/15oz can chopped tomatoes
10ml/2 tsp yeast extract
1 bay leaf

For the topping
450g/1 lb potatoes, peeled and cut into
    large chunks
450g/1 lb parsnips, peeled and cut into
    large chunks
60ml/4 tbsp low-fat natural yogurt
45ml/3 tbsp snipped chives
20ml/4 tsp freshly grated Parmesan
    cheese
2 tomatoes, sliced
25g/1oz/¼ cup pine nuts (optional)

1 Place the lentils in a pan and pour in cold water to cover. Bring to the boil, then boil for 10 minutes.

2 Meanwhile, brown the beef in a saucepan, without any extra fat. Stir in the onion, celery, carrot and garlic. Cook gently for 5 minutes, then stir in the tomatoes.

3 Drain the lentils, reserving 300ml/ ½ pint/1¼ cups of the cooking water in a measuring jug. Add the lentils to the meat mixture, then dissolve the yeast extract in the cooking water and stir it in. Add the bay leaf and bring to the boil, then lower the heat, cover the pan and cook gently for 20 minutes.

NUTRITION NOTES	
Per portion:	
Energy	470Kcals/1985kJ
Fat	10.6g
Saturated fat	2.17g
Cholesterol	36.3mg
Fibre	13.3g

4 Make the topping. Bring a saucepan of lightly salted water to the boil and cook the potatoes and parsnips for about 15 minutes, until tender. Drain, top into a bowl, and mash with the yogurt and chives. Preheat the grill.

5 Remove the bay leaf and divide the mixture among four small dishes. Spoon over the potato mixture. Sprinkle with Parmesan and garnish with tomato slices. Scatter pine nuts over the top, if using, and grill the pies for a few minutes until the topping is crisp and golden.

SAUSAGE BEANPOT WITH DUMPLINGS

Sausages needn't be totally banned on a low fat diet, but choose them carefully. If you are unable to find a reduced-fat variety, choose turkey sausages instead, and always drain off any fat during cooking.

INGREDIENTS

Serves 4
450g/1 lb half-fat sausages
1 medium onion, thinly sliced
1 green pepper, seeded and diced
1 small red chilli, sliced, or 2.5ml/½ tsp
  chilli sauce
400g/14oz can chopped tomatoes
250ml/8 fl oz/1 cup beef stock
425g/15oz can red kidney beans,
  drained
salt and black pepper

For the dumplings
275g/10oz/2½ cups plain flour
10ml/2 tsp baking powder
225g/8oz/1 cup cottage cheese

1 Fry the sausages without fat in a non-stick pan until brown. Add the onion and pepper. Stir in the chilli, tomatoes and stock; bring to the boil.

NUTRITION NOTES

Per portion:
Energy	574Kcals/2409kJ
Fat	13.09g
Saturated fat	0.15g
Cholesterol	52.31mg
Fibre	9.59g

2 Cover and simmer gently for 15–20 minutes, then add the beans and bring to the boil.

3 To make the dumplings, sift the flour and baking powder together and add enough water to mix to a firm dough. Roll out thinly and stamp out 16–18 rounds using a 7.5cm/3in cutter.

4 Place a small spoonful of cottage cheese on each round and bring the edges of the dough together, pinching to enclose. Arrange the dumplings over the sausages in the pan, cover the pan and simmer for 10–12 minutes, until the dumplings are well risen. Serve hot.

HONEY-ROAST PORK WITH HERBS

Herbs and honey add flavour and sweetness to tenderloin – the leanest cut of pork.

INGREDIENTS

Serves 4
450g/1 lb pork tenderloin
30ml/2 tbsp thick honey
30ml/2 tbsp Dijon mustard
5ml/1 tsp chopped fresh rosemary
2.5ml/½ tsp chopped fresh thyme
1.5ml/¼ tsp whole tropical peppercorns
fresh rosemary and thyme sprigs,
*   to garnish*
potato gratin and cauliflower, to serve

For the red onion confit
4 red onions
350ml/12fl oz/1½ cups vegetable stock
15ml/1 tbsp red wine vinegar
15ml/1 tbsp caster sugar
1 garlic clove, crushed
30ml/2 tbsp ruby port
pinch of salt

1 Pre-heat the oven to 180°C/350°F/ Gas 4. Trim off any visible fat from the pork. Put the honey, mustard, rosemary and thyme in a small bowl and mix them together well.

2 Crush the peppercorns using a pestle and mortar. Spread the honey mixture over the pork and sprinkle with the crushed peppercorns. Place in a non-stick roasting tin and cook in the pre-heated oven for 35–45 minutes.

3 For the red onion confit, slice the onions into rings and put them into a heavy-based saucepan.

4 Add the stock, vinegar, sugar and garlic clove to the saucepan. Bring to the boil, then reduce the heat. Cover and simmer for 15 minutes.

5 Uncover and pour in the port and continue to simmer, stirring occasionally, until the onions are soft and the juices thick and syrupy. Season to taste with salt.

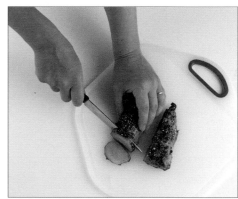

6 Cut the pork into slices and arrange on four warmed plates. Serve garnished with rosemary and thyme and accompanied with the red onion confit, potato gratin and cauliflower.

NUTRITION NOTES	
Per portion:	
Energy	258Kcals/1080kJ
Fat	8.9g
Saturated fat	2.92g
Cholesterol	77.6mg
Fibre	1.2g

TURKEY AND MACARONI CHEESE

A tasty low fat alternative to macaroni cheese, the addition of turkey rashers ensures this dish is a family favourite. Serve with warm ciabatta bread and a mixed leaf salad.

NUTRITION NOTES

Per portion:

Energy	152Kcals/637kJ
Fat	2.8g
Saturated fat	0.7g
Cholesterol	12mg
Fibre	1.1g

INGREDIENTS

Serves 4

1 medium onion, chopped
150ml/¼ pint/⅔ cup vegetable or
  chicken stock
25g/1oz/2 tbsp low fat margarine
45ml/3 tbsp plain flour
300ml/½ pint/¼ cup skimmed milk
50g/2oz reduced fat Cheddar
  cheese, grated
5ml/1 tsp dry mustard
225g/8oz quick-cook macaroni
4 smoked turkey rashers, cut in half
2–3 firm tomatoes, sliced
a few fresh basil leaves
15ml/1 tbsp grated Parmesan cheese
salt and black pepper

1 Put the chopped onion and stock into a non-stick frying pan. Bring to the boil, stirring occasionally and cook for 5–6 minutes or until the stock has reduced entirely and the onion is transparent.

2 Put the margarine, flour, milk and seasoning into a saucepan and whisk together over the heat until thickened and smooth. Draw aside and add the cheese, mustard and onion.

3 Cook the macaroni in a large pan of boiling, salted water according to the instructions on the packet. Preheat the grill. Drain thoroughly and stir into the sauce. Transfer to a shallow oven-proof dish.

4 Arrange the turkey rashers and tomatoes overlapping on top of the macaroni cheese. Tuck in the basil leaves, then sprinkle with Parmesan and grill to lightly brown the top.

THAI CHICKEN AND VEGETABLE STIR-FRY

INGREDIENTS

Serves 4

1 piece lemon grass (or the rind of
   ¹/₂ lemon)
1cm/¹/₂in piece fresh root ginger
1 large garlic clove
30ml/2 tbsp sunflower oil
275g/10oz lean chicken,
   thinly sliced
¹/₂ red pepper, seeded and
   sliced
¹/₂ green pepper, seeded and sliced
4 spring onions, chopped
2 medium carrots, cut into matchsticks
115g/4oz fine green beans
25g/1oz peanuts, lightly crushed
30 ml/2 tbsp oyster sauce
pinch of sugar
salt and black pepper
coriander leaves, to garnish

NUTRITION NOTES

Per portion:

Energy	203Kcals/849kJ
Fat	11.0g
Saturated fat	2.0g
Cholesterol	29.6mg
Fibre	2.6g

1 Thinly slice the lemon grass or lemon rind. Peel and chop the ginger and garlic. Heat the oil in a frying pan over a high heat. Add the lemon grass or lemon rind, ginger and garlic, and stir-fry for 30 seconds until brown.

2 Add the chicken and stir-fry for 2 minutes. Then add all the vegetables and stir-fry for 4–5 minutes, until the chicken is cooked and the vegetables are almost cooked.

3 Finally, stir in the peanuts, oyster sauce, sugar and seasoning to taste. Stir-fry for another minute to blend the flavours. Serve at once, sprinkled with the coriander leaves and accompanied by rice.

COOK'S TIP
Make this quick supper dish a little hotter by adding more fresh root ginger, if liked.

Barbecued Chicken

Serves 4 or 8

8 small chicken pieces
2 limes, cut into wedges, 2 red chillies,
  finely sliced, and 2 lemon grass
  stalks, to garnish
rice, to serve

For the marinade

2 lemon grass stalks, chopped
2.5cm/1in piece fresh root ginger
6 garlic cloves
4 shallots
1/2 bunch coriander roots
15ml/1 tbsp palm sugar
120ml/4fl oz/1/2 cup coconut milk
30ml/2 tbsp fish sauce
30ml/2 tbsp soy sauce

Cook's Tip
Don't eat the skin of the chicken –
it's only left on to keep the flesh
moist during cooking. Coconut
milk makes a good base for a
marinade or sauce, as it is low in
calories and fat.

Nutrition Notes

Per portion (for 8):

Energy	100Kcals/420kJ
Fat	2.8g
Saturated fat	0.89g
Cholesterol	35.6mg
Fibre	0.3g

---

1 To make the marinade, put all the ingredients into a food processor and process until smooth.

2 Put the chicken pieces in a dish and pour over the marinade. Leave in a cool place to marinate for at least 4 hours or overnight.

3 Preheat the oven to 200°C/400°F/ Gas 6. Put the chicken pieces on a rack on a baking tray. Brush with marinade and bake in the oven for about 20–30 minutes or until the chicken is cooked and golden brown. Turn the pieces over halfway through and brush with more marinade.

4 Garnish with lime wedges, finely sliced red chillies and lemon grass stalks. Serve with rice.

HOT CHICKEN CURRY

This curry has a flavourful thick sauce, and includes red and green peppers for extra colour. Serve with wholemeal chapatis or plain boiled rice.

INGREDIENTS

Serves 4
30ml/2 tbsp corn oil
1.5ml/¼ tsp fenugreek seeds
1.5ml/¼ tsp onion seeds
2 onions, chopped
1 garlic clove, crushed
2.5ml/½ tsp grated fresh root ginger
5ml/1 tsp ground coriander
5ml/1 tsp chilli powder
5ml/1 tsp salt
400g/14oz can tomatoes
30ml/2 tbsp lemon juice
350g/12oz chicken without skin and
  bone, cubed
30ml/2 tbsp chopped fresh coriander
3 green chillies, chopped
½ red pepper, cut into chunks
½ green pepper, cut into chunks
fresh coriander leaves, to garnish

1 Heat the oil in a medium saucepan, and fry the fenugreek and onion seeds until they turn a shade darker. Add the onions, garlic and ginger and fry for about 5 minutes until the onions are golden. Lower the heat to very low.

COOK'S TIP
For a milder version of this delicious curry, simply omit some or all of the fresh green chillies.

2 Meanwhile, in a separate bowl, mix together the ground coriander, chilli powder, salt, tomatoes and lemon juice.

3 Pour this mixture into the pan and turn up the heat to medium. Stir-fry for about 3 minutes.

NUTRITION NOTES	
Per portion:	
Energy	216Kcals/900kJ
Fat	10.0g
Saturated fat	2.06g
Cholesterol	49.9mg
Fibre	2.2g

4 Add the chicken and stir-fry for about 5–7 minutes. Take care not to overcook the chicken.

5 Add the fresh coriander, green chillies and the pepper chunks. Lower the heat, cover, and simmer for about 10 minutes until cooked. Serve hot, garnished with fresh coriander leaves.

FISH AND SEAFOOD

Fish is ideally designed for healthy, quick, tasty meals. Most types of fish are very low in fat and high in protein, and even oily fish is high in essential fatty acids that boost 'good' HDL cholesterol. Furthermore, some fish, such as prawns, though high in cholesterol, are low in fats, and it is now believed that it is the amount of saturated fat in the diet that most affects blood cholesterol levels. Healthy, and easy to cook, fish is perfect for absorbing the exotic flavours of different herbs, spices and marinades—try Glazed Garlic Prawns with its refreshing tangy lemon and mango chutney sauce for a delicious, healthy meal.

HADDOCK AND BROCCOLI CHOWDER

A warming main-meal soup for hearty appetites.

INGREDIENTS

Serves 4

4 spring onions, sliced
450g/1 lb new potatoes, diced
300ml/½ pint/1¼ cups fish stock or
*   water*
300ml/½ pint/1¼ cups skimmed milk
1 bay leaf
225g/8oz/2 cups broccoli florets, sliced
450g/1 lb smoked haddock fillets,
*   skinned*
198g/7oz can sweetcorn, drained
black pepper
chopped spring onions, to garnish

1 Place the spring onions and potatoes in a large saucepan and add the stock, milk and bay leaf. Bring the soup to the boil, then cover the pan and simmer for 10 minutes.

2 Add the broccoli to the pan. Cut the fish into bite-sized chunks and add to the pan with the sweetcorn.

3 Season the soup well with black pepper, then cover the pan and simmer for a further 5 minutes, or until the fish is cooked through. Remove the bay leaf and scatter over the spring onion. Serve hot, with crusty bread.

COOK'S TIP
When new potatoes are not available, old ones can be used, but choose a waxy variety which will not disintegrate.

NUTRITION NOTES

Per portion:

Energy	268Kcals/1124kJ
Fat	2.19g
Saturated fat	0.27g
Cholesterol	57.75mg
Fibre	3.36g

TUNA AND CORN FISH CAKES

These economical little tuna fish cakes are quick to make. Either use fresh mashed potatoes, or make a storecupboard version with instant mash.

INGREDIENTS

Serves 4

*300g/11oz/1¼ cups cooked mashed
    potatoes*
*200g/7oz can tuna fish in soya oil,
    drained*
*115g/4oz/¾ cup canned or frozen
    sweetcorn*
30ml/2 tbsp chopped fresh parsley
*50g/2oz/1 cup fresh white or brown
    breadcrumbs*
salt and black pepper
lemon wedges, to serve

1 Place the mashed potato in a bowl and stir in the tuna fish, sweetcorn and chopped parsley.

2 Season to taste with salt and pepper, then shape into eight patty shapes with your hands.

3 Spread out the breadcrumbs on a plate and press the fish cakes into the breadcrumbs to coat lightly, then place on a baking sheet.

4 Cook the fish cakes under a moderately hot grill until crisp and golden brown, turning once. Serve hot with lemon wedges and fresh vegetables.

COOK'S TIP
For simple storecupboard variations which are just as nutritious, try using canned sardines, red or pink salmon, or smoked mackerel in place of the tuna.

NUTRITION NOTES

Per portion:

Energy	203Kcals/852kJ
Fat	4.62g
Saturated fat	0.81g
Cholesterol	21.25mg
Fibre	1.82g

FISH FILLETS WITH A CHILLI SAUCE

Fish fillets, marinated with fresh coriander and lemon juice, then grilled and served with a chilli sauce, are delicious accompanied with saffron rice.

INGREDIENTS

Serves 4

4 flatfish fillets, such as plaice, sole or flounder, about 115g/4oz each
30ml/2 tbsp lemon juice
15ml/1 tbsp finely chopped fresh coriander
15ml/1 tbsp vegetable oil
lime wedges and coriander leaves, to garnish

For the sauce

5ml/1 tsp grated fresh root ginger
30ml/2 tbsp tomato purée
5ml/1 tsp sugar
5ml/1 tsp salt
15ml/1 tbsp chilli sauce
15ml/1 tbsp malt vinegar
300ml/½ pint/1¼ cups water

1 Rinse, pat dry and place the fish fillets in a medium bowl. Add the lemon juice, fresh coriander and oil and rub into the fish. Leave to marinate for at least 1 hour. The flavour will improve if you can leave it for longer.

2 To make the sauce, mix together all the sauce ingredients, pour into a small saucepan and simmer over a low heat for about 6 minutes, stirring occasionally.

3 Preheat the grill to medium. Cook the fillets under the grill for about 5–7 minutes.

4 When the fillets are cooked, remove and arrange them on a warmed serving dish.

5 The chilli sauce should now be fairly thick – about the consistency of a thick chicken soup.

6 Spoon the sauce over the fillets, garnish with the lime wedges and coriander leaves, and serve with rice.

NUTRITION NOTES

Per portion:

Energy	142Kcals/599kJ
Fat	5.3g
Saturated fat	0.75g
Cholesterol	48.3mg
Fibre	0.2g

GLAZED GARLIC PRAWNS

A fairly simple and quick dish to prepare, it is best to peel the prawns as this helps them to absorb maximum flavour. Serve as a main course with a variety of accompaniments, or with a salad as a starter.

INGREDIENTS

Serves 4

15ml/1 tbsp sunflower oil
3 garlic cloves, roughly chopped
3 tomatoes, chopped
2.5ml/½ tsp salt
5ml/1 tsp crushed dried red chillies
5ml/1 tsp lemon juice
15ml/1 tbsp mango chutney
1 green chilli, chopped
15–20 cooked king prawns, peeled
fresh coriander leaves and 2 chopped
   spring onions, to garnish

NUTRITION NOTES

Per portion:

Energy	101Kcals/421kJ
Fat	3.6g
Saturated fat	0.41g
Cholesterol	95.0mg
Fibre	0.9g

1 Heat the oil in a medium saucepan, and add the chopped garlic.

2 Lower the heat. Add the chopped tomatoes along with the salt, crushed chillies, lemon juice, mango chutney and chopped fresh chilli.

3 Finally add the prawns, turn up the heat and stir-fry quickly until they are heated through.

4 Transfer to a serving dish. Serve immediately garnished with fresh coriander leaves and chopped spring onions.

COD CREOLE

INGREDIENTS

Serves 4

450g/1 lb cod fillets, skinned
15ml/1 tbsp lime or lemon juice
10ml/2 tsp olive oil
1 medium onion, finely chopped
1 green pepper, seeded and sliced
2.5ml/½ tsp cayenne pepper
2.5ml/½ tsp garlic salt
400g/14oz can chopped tomatoes

NUTRITION NOTES

Per portion:

Energy	130Kcals/546kJ
Fat	2.61g
Saturated fat	0.38g
Cholesterol	51.75mg
Fibre	1.61g

1 Cut the cod fillets into bite-sized chunks and sprinkle with the lime or lemon juice.

2 In a large, non-stick pan, heat the olive oil and fry the onion and pepper gently until softened. Add the cayenne pepper and garlic salt.

3 Stir in the cod with the chopped tomatoes. Bring to the boil, then cover and simmer for about 5 minutes, or until the fish flakes easily. Serve with boiled rice or potatoes.

FIVE-SPICE FISH

Chinese mixtures of spicy, sweet and sour flavours are particularly successful with fish, and dinner is ready in minutes.

INGREDIENTS

Serves 4

4 white fish fillets,such as cod, haddock
  or hoki (about 175g/6oz each)
5ml/1 tsp Chinese five-spice powder
20ml/4 tsp cornflour
15ml/1 tbsp sesame or sunflower oil
3 spring onions, shredded
5ml/1 tsp finely chopped root ginger
150g/5oz button mushrooms, sliced
115g/4oz baby corn cobs, sliced
30ml/2 tbsp soy sauce
45ml/3 tbsp dry sherry or apple juice
5ml/1 tsp sugar
salt and black pepper

1 Toss the fish in the five-spice powder and cornflour to coat.

2 Heat the oil in a frying pan or wok and stir-fry the onions, ginger mushrooms and corn cobs for about 1 minute. Add the fish and cook for 2–3 minutes, turning once.

3 Mix together the soy sauce, sherry and sugar then pour over the fish. Simmer for 2 minutes, adjust the seasoning, then serve with noodles and stir-fried vegetables.

NUTRITION NOTES

Per portion:

Energy	213Kcals/893kJ
Fat	4.41g
Saturated fat	0.67g
Cholesterol	80.5mg
Fibre	1.08g

PRAWNS WITH VEGETABLES

This is a light and nutritious dish. It is excellent served either on a bed of lettuce leaves, with plain boiled rice or wholemeal chapatis for a healthy meal.

INGREDIENTS

Serves 4
30ml/2 tbsp chopped fresh coriander
5ml/1 tsp salt
2 green chillies, seeded if required
45ml/3 tbsp lemon juice
30ml/2 tbsp vegetable oil
20 cooked king prawns, peeled
1 courgette, thickly sliced
1 onion, cut into 8 chunks
8 cherry tomatoes
8 baby corn
mixed salad leaves, to serve

NUTRITION NOTES

Per portion:
Energy	142Kcals/592kJ
Fat	6.6g
Saturated fat	0.68g
Cholesterol	125.4mg
Fibre	1.2g

1 Place the chopped coriander, salt, green chillies, lemon juice and oil in a food processor or blender and process for a few seconds.

2 Remove the paste from the processor and transfer to a mixing bowl.

3 Add the peeled prawns to the paste and stir to make sure that all the prawns are well coated. Set aside to marinate for about 30 minutes.

4 Preheat the grill to very hot, then turn the heat down to medium.

5 Arrange the vegetables and prawns alternately on four skewers. When all the skewers are ready place them under the preheated grill for about 5–7 minutes until cooked and browned.

6 Serve immediately on a bed of mixed salad leaves.

COOK'S TIP
King prawns are a luxury, but worth choosing for a very special dinner party. For a more economical variation, substitute the king prawns with 450g/1 lb/2½ cups peeled prawns.

TUNA FISH AND FLAGEOLET BEAN SALAD

Two cans of tuna fish form the basis of this delicious and easy-to-make storecupboard salad.

INGREDIENTS

Serves 4

90ml/6 tbsp reduced calorie
  mayonnaise
5ml/1 tsp mustard
30ml/2 tbsp capers
45ml/3 tbsp chopped fresh parsley
pinch of celery salt
2 x 200g/7oz cans tuna fish in brine,
  drained
3 little gem lettuces
400g/14oz can flageolet beans, drained
12 cherry tomatoes, halved
400g/14oz can baby artichoke hearts,
  halved
toasted sesame bread or sticks, to serve

NUTRITION NOTES

Per portion:
Energy	299Kcals/1255kJ
Fat	13.91g
Saturated fat	2.12g
Cholesterol	33mg
Fibre	6.36g

1 Combine the mayonnaise, mustard, capers and parsley in a mixing bowl. Season to taste with celery salt.

2 Flake the tuna into the dressing and toss gently.

3 Arrange the lettuce leaves on four plates, then spoon the tuna mixture on to the leaves.

COOK'S TIP
If flageolet beans are not available, use cannellini beans.

4 Spoon the flageolet beans to one side, followed by the tomatoes and artichoke hearts.

5 Serve with slices of toasted sesame bread or sticks.

VEGETABLES AND SALADS

We're very lucky to have a huge variety of fresh vegetables available all year round these days, so there is no excuse for not making maximum use of them at every opportunity, whether they form the basis of the main course, or are served as an accompaniment to meat or fish dishes. Be adventurous with vegetables: use them in different combinations or with exotic herbs and spices for new textures and flavours. Middle-Eastern Vegetable Stew with cumin and fresh mint is just one example. Take a fresh look at salads, too, and discover that they needn't be soaked in heavy, oily dressings to be tasty. Try tangy, yogurt dressings, cider vinegar and fromage frais.

SPICY JACKET POTATOES

Serves 2–4

2 large baking potatoes
5ml/1 tsp sunflower oil
1 small onion, finely chopped
2.5cm/1in piece fresh ginger root, grated
5ml/1 tsp ground cumin
5ml/1 tsp ground coriander
2.5ml/½ tsp ground turmeric
garlic salt
natural yogurt and fresh coriander
  sprigs, to serve

1 Preheat the oven to 190°C/375°F/ Gas 5. Prick the potatoes with a fork. Bake for 40 minutes, or until soft.

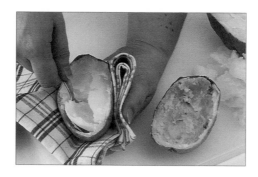

2 Cut the potatoes in half and scoop out the flesh. Heat the oil in a non-stick pan and fry the onion for a few minutes to soften. Stir in the ginger, cumin, coriander and turmeric.

3 Stir over a low heat for about 2 minutes, then add the potato flesh, and garlic salt, to taste.

4 Cook the potato mixture for a further 2 minutes, stirring occasionally. Spoon the mixture back into the potato shells and top each with a spoonful of natural yogurt and a sprig or two of fresh coriander. Serve hot.

NUTRITION NOTES

Per portion:
Energy	212Kcals/890kJ
Fat	2.54g
Saturated fat	0.31g
Cholesterol	0.4mg
Fibre	3.35g

TWO BEANS PROVENÇAL

Serves 4

5ml/1 tsp olive oil
1 small onion, finely chopped
1 garlic clove, crushed
225g/8oz French beans
225g/8oz runner beans
2 tomatoes, skinned and chopped
salt and black pepper

NUTRITION NOTES

Per portion:
Energy	68Kcals/286kJ
Fat	1.76g
Saturated fat	0.13g
Cholesterol	0
Fibre	5.39g

1 Heat the oil in a heavy-based, or non-stick, pan and sauté the chopped onion over a medium heat until softened but not browned.

2 Add the garlic, the French and runner beans and the tomatoes, then season well and cover tightly.

3 Cook over a fairly low heat, shaking the pan occasionally, for about 30 minutes, or until the beans are tender. Serve hot.

SWEET POTATO AND CARROT SALAD

INGREDIENTS

Serves 4

1 sweet potato, peeled and roughly diced
2 carrots, cut into thick diagonal slices
3 tomatoes
8–10 iceberg lettuce leaves
75g/3oz/³⁄₄ cup canned chick-peas, drained

For the dressing
15ml/1 tbsp clear honey
90ml/6 tbsp low fat natural yogurt
2.5ml/¹⁄₂ tsp salt
5ml/1 tsp coarsely ground black pepper

For the garnish
15ml/1 tbsp walnuts
15ml/1 tbsp sultanas
1 small onion, cut into rings

NUTRITION NOTES

Per portion:
Energy	147Kcals/614kJ
Fat	3.8g
Saturated fat	0.52g
Cholesterol	1.2mg
Fibre	3.4g

1 Place the potatoes in a large saucepan and cover with water. Bring to the boil and cook until soft but not mushy, cover the pan and set aside. Boil the carrots for a few minutes making sure they remain crunchy. Add to the sweet potatoes.

3 Slice the tops off the tomatoes, then scoop out and discard the seeds. Roughly chop the flesh.

5 For the dressing, blend together all the ingredients and beat together with a fork.

2 Drain the water from the sweet potatoes and carrots, and place together in a bowl.

4 Line a glass bowl with the lettuce leaves. Mix together the sweet potatoes, carrots, chick-peas and tomatoes, and place in the bowl.

6 Spoon the dressing over the salad or serve it in a separate bowl, if desired. Garnish the salad with the walnuts, sultanas and onion rings.

LEMONY VEGETABLE PARCELS

INGREDIENTS

Serves 4

2 medium carrots
1 small swede
1 large parsnip
1 leek, sliced
finely grated rind of ½ lemon
15ml/1 tbsp lemon juice
15ml/1 tbsp wholegrain mustard
5ml/1 tsp walnut or sunflower oil
salt and black pepper

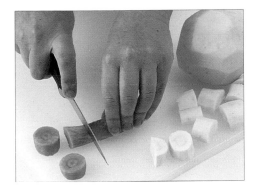

1 Preheat the oven to 190°C/375°F/ Gas 5. Peel the root vegetables and cut into 1cm/½ in cubes. Place in a large bowl, then add the sliced leek.

2 Stir the lemon rind and juice and the mustard into the vegetables and mix well, then season to taste.

3 Cut four 30cm/12 in squares of non-stick baking paper and brush lightly with the oil.

4 Divide the vegetables among them. Roll up the paper from one side, then twist the ends firmly to seal.

5 Place the parcels on a baking sheet and bake for 50–55 minutes, or until the vegetables are just tender. Serve hot with roast or grilled meats.

NUTRITION NOTES	
Per portion	
Energy	78Kcals/326kJ
Fat	2.06g
Saturated fat	0.08g
Cholesterol	0
Fibre	5.15g

Middle-Eastern Vegetable Stew

A spiced dish of mixed vegetables which can be served as a side dish or as a vegetarian main course. Children may prefer less chilli.

Ingredients

Serves 4–6
45ml/3 tbsp vegetable or chicken stock
1 green pepper, seeded and sliced
2 medium courgettes, sliced
2 medium carrots, sliced
2 celery sticks, sliced
2 medium potatoes, diced
400g/14oz can chopped tomatoes
5ml/1 tsp chilli powder
30ml/2 tbsp chopped fresh mint
15ml/1 tbsp ground cumin
400g/14oz can chick-peas, drained
salt and black pepper
mint sprigs, to garnish

1 Heat the vegetable or chicken stock in a large flameproof casserole until boiling, then add the sliced pepper, courgettes, carrot and celery. Stir over a high heat for 2–3 minutes, until the vegetables are just beginning to soften.

2 Add the potatoes, tomatoes, chilli powder, mint and cumin. Add the chick-peas and bring to the boil.

3 Reduce the heat, cover the casserole and simmer for 30 minutes, or until all the vegetables are tender. Season to taste with salt and pepper and serve hot garnished with mint leaves.

Cook's Tip
Chick-peas are traditional in this type of Middle-Eastern dish, but if you prefer, red kidney beans or haricot beans can be used instead.

Nutrition Notes

Per portion:
Energy	168Kcals/703kJ
Fat	3.16g
Saturated fat	0.12g
Cholesterol	0
Fibre	6.13g

SUMMER VEGETABLE BRAISE

Tender, young vegetables are ideal for quick cooking in a minimum of liquid. Use any mixture of the family's favourite vegetables, as long as they are of similar size.

INGREDIENTS

Serves 4

175g/6oz/2½ cups baby carrots
175g/6oz/2 cups sugar-snap peas or
mangetout
115g/4oz/1¼ cups baby corn cobs
90ml/6 tbsp vegetable stock
10ml/2 tsp lime juice
salt and black pepper
chopped fresh parsley parsley and
snipped fresh chives, to garnish

1 Place the carrots, peas and baby corn cobs in a large heavy-based saucepan with the vegetable stock and lime juice. Bring to the boil.

2 Cover the pan and reduce the heat, then simmer for 6–8 minutes, shaking the pan occasionally, until the vegetables are just tender.

3 Season the vegetables to taste with salt and pepper, then stir in the chopped fresh parsley and snipped chives. Cook the vegetables for a few seconds more, stirring them once or twice until the herbs are well mixed, then serve at once with grilled lamb chops or roast chicken.

COOK'S TIP
You can make this dish in the winter too, but cut larger, tougher vegetables into chunks and cook for slightly longer.

NUTRITION NOTES

Per portion:

Energy	36Kcals/152kJ
Fat	0.45g
Saturated fat	0
Cholesterol	0
Fibre	2.35g

ROSEMARY ROASTIES

These unusual roast potatoes use far less fat than traditional roast potatoes, and because they still have their skins they not only absorb less oil but have more flavour too.

INGREDIENTS

Serves 4
1kg/2 lb small red potatoes
10ml/2 tsp walnut or sunflower oil
30ml/2 tbsp fresh rosemary leaves
salt and paprika

1 Preheat the oven to 240°C/475°F/ Gas 9. Leave the potatoes whole with the peel on, or if large, cut in half. Place the potatoes in a large pan of cold water and bring to the boil. Drain well.

2 Drizzle the walnut or sunflower oil over the potatoes and shake the pan to coat them evenly.

3 Tip the potatoes into a shallow roasting tin. Sprinkle with rosemary, salt and paprika. Roast for 30 minutes or until crisp. Serve hot.

NUTRITION NOTES

Per portion:
Energy	205Kcals/865kJ
Fat	2.22g
Saturated fat	0.19g
Cholesterol	0
Fibre	3.25g

BAKED COURGETTES IN PASSATA

INGREDIENTS

Serves 4
5ml/1 tsp olive oil
3 large courgettes, thinly sliced
½ small red onion, finely chopped
300ml/½ pint/1¼ cups passata
30ml/2 tbsp chopped fresh thyme
garlic salt and black pepper
fresh thyme sprigs, to garnish

1 Preheat the oven to 190°C/375°F/ Gas 5. Brush an ovenproof dish with olive oil. Arrange half the courgettes and onion in the dish.

2 Spoon half the passata over the vegetables and sprinkle with some of the fresh thyme, then season to taste with garlic salt and pepper.

3 Arrange the remaining courgettes and onion in the dish on top of the passata, then season to taste with more garlic salt and pepper. Spoon over the remaining passata and spread evenly.

4 Cover the dish with foil, then bake for 40–45 minutes, or until the courgettes are tender. Garnish with sprigs of thyme and serve hot.

NUTRITION NOTES

Per portion:
Energy	49Kcals/205kJ
Fat	1.43g
Saturated fat	0.22g
Cholesterol	0
Fibre	1.73g

Red Cabbage in Port and Red Wine

A sweet and sour, spicy red cabbage dish, with the added crunch of walnuts.

Ingredients

Serves 6
15ml/1 tbsp walnut oil
1 onion, sliced
2 whole star anise
5ml/1 tsp ground cinnamon
pinch of ground cloves
450g/1 lb/5 cups, finely shredded red cabbage
30ml/2 tbsp dark brown sugar
45ml/3 tbsp red wine vinegar
300ml/½ pint/1¼ cups red wine
150ml/¼ pint/⅔ cup port
2 pears, cut into 1cm/½ in cubes
115g/4oz/⅔ cup raisins
115g/4oz/½ cup walnut halves
salt and black pepper

Nutrition Notes	
Per portion:	
Energy	336Kcals/1409kJ
Fat	15.41g
Saturated fat	1.58g
Cholesterol	0
Fibre	4.31g

1 Heat the oil in a large flameproof casserole. Add the onion and cook gently for about 5 minutes until softened.

2 Add the star anise, cinnamon, cloves and cabbage, and cook for a further 3 minutes.

3 Stir in the sugar, vinegar, red wine and port. Cover the pan and simmer gently for a further 10 minutes, stirring occasionally.

4 Stir in the cubed pears and raisins, and cook for a further 10 minutes or until the cabbage is tender. Season to taste. Mix in the walnut halves and serve immediately.

Cook's Tip
If you are unable to buy pre-packaged walnut halves, buy whole ones and cut them in half.

WATERCRESS POTATO SALAD BOWL

New potatoes are equally good hot or cold, and this colourful, nutritious salad is an ideal way of making the most of them.

INGREDIENTS

Serves 4

450g/1 lb small new potatoes, unpeeled
1 bunch watercress
200g/7oz/1½ cups cherry tomatoes, halved
30ml/2 tbsp pumpkin seeds
45ml/3 tbsp low fat fromage frais
15ml/1 tbsp cider vinegar
5ml/1 tsp soft light brown sugar
salt and paprika

1 Cook the potatoes in lightly salted, boiling water until just tender, then drain and leave to cool.

2 Toss together the potatoes, watercress, tomatoes and pumpkin seeds.

3 Place the fromage frais, vinegar, sugar, salt and paprika in a screw-topped jar and shake well to mix. Pour over the salad just before serving.

NUTRITION NOTES

Per portion:

Energy	150Kcals/630kJ
Fat	4.15g
Saturated fat	0.81g
Cholesterol	0.11mg
Fibre	2.55g

COOK'S TIP
If you are packing this salad for a picnic, take the dressing in the jar and toss in just before serving.

DESSERTS, CAKES AND BAKES

Dessert lovers will be glad to learn that desserts need not be taboo in low-fat and low cholesterol diets. There are lots of ways to cook delicious desserts, cakes and bakes without the need for rich, high-fat mixtures. The rapidly expanding range of low-fat dairy products such as fromage frais, yogurt and crème fraîche means that lighter, far less rich desserts are now possible—without sacrificing enjoyment. Classic dishes can be made a little less sinful by addng less fat and more flavour through the addition of nuts, fruits and spices—try Sunflower Sultana Scones and Apricot and Orange Roulade.

GOLDEN GINGER COMPÔTE

Warm, spicy and full of sun-ripened ingredients – this is the perfect winter dessert.

INGREDIENTS

Serves 4
200g/7oz/2 cups kumquats
200g/7oz/1¼ cups dried apricots
30ml/2 tbsp sultanas
400ml/14fl oz/1⅔ cups water
1 orange
2.5cm/1 in piece fresh root ginger
4 cardamom pods
4 cloves
30ml/2 tbsp clear honey
15ml/1 tbsp flaked almonds, toasted

NUTRITION NOTES

Per portion:
Energy	196Kcals/825kJ
Fat	2.84g
Saturated fat	0.41g
Cholesterol	0
Fibre	6.82g

2 Pare the rind thinly from the orange, peel and grate the ginger, crush the cardamom pods and add to the pan, with the cloves.

3 Reduce the heat, cover the pan and simmer gently for about 30 minutes, or until the fruit is tender.

1 Wash the kumquats and, if they are large, cut them in half. Place them in a saucepan with the apricots, sultanas and water. Bring to the boil.

4 Squeeze the juice from the orange and add to the pan with honey to sweeten to taste, sprinkle with flaked almonds, and serve warm.

VARIATION
Use ready-to-eat dried apricots, but reduce the liquid to 300ml/½ pint/1¼ cups, and add 5 minutes before the end.

BAKED APPLES IN HONEY AND LEMON

A classic mix of flavours in a
healthy, traditional family
pudding. Serve warm, with
skimmed-milk custard.

INGREDIENTS

Serves 4
4 cooking apples
15ml/1 tbsp clear honey
grated rind and juice of 1 lemon
25g/1oz/2 tbsp low fat margarine

NUTRITION NOTES

Per portion:
Energy	71Kcals/299kJ
Fat	1.69g
Saturated fat	0.37g
Cholesterol	0.23mg
Fibre	1.93g

VARIATION
Apples are divided into dessert (or
eating) and cooking apples. While
cooking apples can only be used
for culinary purposes because they
have a sour taste, some dessert
apples, especially if firm, can be
used in cooking. Look for
smooth-skinned apples and avoid
any with brown bruises.

1 Preheat the oven to 180°C/350°F/
Gas 4. Remove the cores from the
apples, leaving them whole.

2 With a canelle or sharp knife, cut
lines through the apple skin at inter-
vals and place in an ovenproof dish.

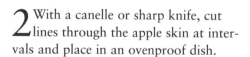

3 Mix together the honey, lemon rind
and juice, and low fat margarine.

4 Spoon the mixture into the apples
and cover the dish with foil or a lid.
Bake for about 40–45 minutes, or until
the apples are tender. Serve with
custard made from skimmed milk.

COOK'S TIP
This recipe can also be cooked in
the microwave to save time. Place
the apples in a microwave-safe
dish and cover them with a lid or
pierced clear film. Microwave on
FULL POWER (100%) for about
9–10 minutes.

FRUITY BREAD PUDDING

A delicious family favourite pud from grandmother's day, with a lighter, healthier touch.

INGREDIENTS

Serves 4

75g/3oz/⅔ cup mixed dried fruit
150ml/¼ pint/⅔ cup apple juice
115g/4oz stale brown or white bread,
  diced
5ml/1 tsp mixed spice
1 large banana, sliced
150ml/¼ pint/⅔ cup skimmed milk
15ml/1 tbsp demerara sugar
natural low fat yogurt, to serve

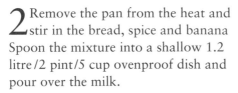

1 Preheat the oven to 200°C/400°F/ Gas 6. Place the dried fruit in a small pan with the apple juice and bring to the boil.

2 Remove the pan from the heat and stir in the bread, spice and banana Spoon the mixture into a shallow 1.2 litre/2 pint/5 cup ovenproof dish and pour over the milk.

3 Sprinkle with demerara sugar and bake for 25–30 minutes, until firm and golden brown. Serve hot or cold with natural yogurt.

COOK'S TIP
Different types of bread will absorb varying amounts of liquid, so you may need to adjust the amount of milk to allow for this.

NUTRITION NOTES

Per portion:

Energy	190Kcals/800kJ
Fat	0.89g
Saturated fat	0.21g
Cholesterol	0.75mg
Fibre	1.8g

BAKED BLACKBERRY CHEESECAKE

This light cheesecake is best made with wild blackberries, but cultivated ones will do. You can also substitute them for other soft fruit such as raspberries or loganberries.

INGREDIENTS

Serves 5

175g/6oz/¾ cup cottage cheese
150g/5oz/⅔ cup low fat natural yogurt
15ml/1 tbsp wholemeal flour
30ml/2 tbsp golden caster sugar
1 egg
1 egg white
finely grated rind and juice of ½ lemon
200g/7oz/2 cups blackberries

NUTRITION NOTES

Per portion:	
Energy	94Kcals/394kJ
Fat	1.67g
Saturated fat	1.03g
Cholesterol	5.75mg
Fibre	1.71g

1 Preheat the oven to 180°C/350°F/ Gas 4. Lightly grease and line the base of an 18cm/7 in cake tin.

2 Whizz the cottage cheese in a food processor or blender until smooth, or rub it through a sieve.

3 Add the yogurt, flour, sugar, egg and egg white, and mix. Add the lemon rind and juice, and blackberries, reserving a few for decoration.

4 Tip the mixture into the prepared tin and bake it for about 30–35 minutes, or until just set. Turn off the oven and leave for 30 minutes.

5 Run a knife around the edge of the cheesecake, and then turn it out.

6 Remove the lining paper and place the cheesecake on a warm serving plate. Decorate with the reserved blackberries and serve it warm.

COOK'S TIP

If you prefer to use canned blackberries, choose those preserved in natural juice and drain the fruit well before adding it to the cheesecake mixture. The juice may be served with the cheesecake, but this will increase the total calories.

Hot Plum Batter

Other fruits can be used in place of plums, depending on the season. Canned black cherries are also a convenient storecupboard substitute.

INGREDIENTS

Serves 4

450g/1 lb ripe red plums, quartered
    and stoned
200ml/7 fl oz/⅞ cup skimmed milk
60ml/4 tbsp skimmed milk powder
15ml/1 tbsp light muscovado sugar
5ml/1 tsp vanilla essence
75g/3oz self-raising flour
2 egg whites
icing sugar, to sprinkle

1 Preheat the oven to 220°C/425°F/ Gas 7. Lightly oil a wide, shallow ovenproof dish and add the plums.

2 Pour the milk, milk powder, sugar, vanilla, flour and egg whites into a food processor. Process until smooth.

3 Pour the batter over the plums. Bake for 25–30 minutes, or until well risen and golden. Sprinkle with icing sugar and serve immediately.

NUTRITION NOTES

Per portion:

Energy	195Kcals/816kJ
Fat	0.48g
Saturated fat	0.12g
Cholesterol	2.8mg
Fibre	2.27g

Glazed Apricot Sponge

Proper puddings are usually very high in saturated fat, but this one uses the minimum of oil and no eggs.

INGREDIENTS

Serves 4

10ml/2 tsp golden syrup
411g/14½oz can apricot halves in
    fruit juice
150g/5oz/1¼ cup self-raising flour
75g/3oz/1½ cups fresh breadcrumbs
90g/3½oz/⅔ cup light muscovado
    sugar
5ml/1 tsp ground cinnamon
30ml/2 tbsp sunflower oil
175ml/6 fl oz/¾ cup skimmed milk

1 Preheat the oven to 180°C/350°F/ Gas 4. Lightly oil a 900ml/1½ pint/3¾ cup pudding basin. Spoon in the syrup.

2 Drain the apricots and reserve the juice. Arrange about 8 halves in the basin. Purée the rest of the apricots with the juice and set aside.

3 Mix the flour, breadcrumbs, sugar and cinnamon then beat in the oil and milk. Spoon into the basin and bake for 50–55 minutes, or until firm and golden. Turn out and serve with the puréed fruit as a sauce.

NUTRITION NOTES

Per portion:

Energy	364Kcals/1530kJ
Fat	6.47g
Saturated fat	0.89g
Cholesterol	0.88mg
Fibre	2.37g

PEARS IN MAPLE AND YOGURT SAUCE

INGREDIENTS

Serves 6
6 firm pears
1 tbsp lemon juice
1 cup sweet white wine or
    sweet cider
thinly pared rind of 1 lemon
1 cinnamon stick
2 tbsp maple syrup
½ tsp arrowroot
⅔ cup plain low fat
    strained yogurt

NUTRITION NOTES

Per portion:

Energy	132Kcals/556kJ
Fat	2.4g
Saturated fat	1.43g
Cholesterol	3.25mg
Fiber	2.64g

1 Thinly peel the pears, leaving them whole and with stalks intact. Brush them with lemon juice, to prevent them from browning. Use a potato peeler or small knife to scoop out the core from the base of each pear.

2 Place the pears in a wide, heavy saucepan and pour over the wine or cider, with enough cold water almost to cover the pears.

3 Add the lemon rind and cinnamon stick, and then bring to a boil. Reduce the heat, and simmer the pears gently for 30–40 minutes, or until tender. Turn the pears occasionally. Lift the pears out carefully, draining them well, and set aside.

4 Bring the pear cooking liquid to a boil and boil uncovered to reduce to about ½ cup.

5 Strain the liquid and add the maple syrup. Blend a little of the liquid with the arrowroot. Return to the pan and cook, stirring, until thick and clear. Leave to cool.

6 Slice each pear about three-quarters of the way through, leaving the slices attached at the stem end. Fan each pear out on a serving plate.

7 Stir 2 tbsp of the cooled syrup into the yogurt and spoon it around the pears. Drizzle with the remaining syrup and serve immediately.

COOK'S TIP
Poach the pears in advance, and have the cooled syrup ready to spoon on to the plates just before serving. The cooking time of this dish will vary, depending upon the type and ripeness of the pears. The pears should be ripe, but still firm – over-ripe ones will not keep their shape well.

RASPBERRY PASSION FRUIT SWIRLS

If passion fruit is not available, this simple dessert can be made with raspberries alone.

INGREDIENTS

Serves 4

300g/11oz/2½ cups raspberries
2 passion fruit
400g/14oz/1⅔ cups low fat fromage frais
30ml/2 tbsp caster sugar
raspberries and sprigs of mint, to decorate

1 Mash the raspberries in a small bowl with a fork until the juice runs. Scoop out the passion fruit pulp into a separate bowl with the fromage frais and sugar and mix well.

3 Decorate each dessert with a whole raspberry and a sprig of fresh mint. Serve chilled.

2 Spoon alternate spoonfuls of the raspberry pulp and the fromage frais mixture into stemmed glasses or one large serving dish, stirring lightly to create a swirled effect.

COOK'S TIP
Over-ripe, slightly soft fruit can also be used in this recipe. Use frozen raspberries when fresh are not available, but thaw first.

NUTRITION NOTES

Per portion:

Energy	110Kcals/462kJ
Fat	0.47g
Saturated fat	0.13g
Cholesterol	1mg
Fibre	2.12g

Cherry Pancakes

Ingredients

Serves 4

50g/2oz/½ cup plain flour
50g/2oz/⅓ cup wholemeal flour
pinch of salt
1 egg white
150ml/¼ pint/⅔ cup skimmed milk
150ml/¼ pint/⅔ cup water
15ml/1 tbsp sunflower oil for frying
low fat fromage frais, to serve

For the filling
425g/15oz can black cherries in juice
7.5ml/1½ tsp arrowroot

Nutrition Notes

Per portion:

Energy	173Kcals/725kJ
Fat	3.33g
Saturated fat	0.44g
Cholesterol	0.75mg
Fibre	2.36g

1 Sift the flours and salt into a bowl, adding any bran left in the sieve to the bowl at the end.

2 Make a well in the centre of the flour and add the egg white. Gradually beat in the milk and water, whisking hard until all the liquid is incorporated and the batter is smooth and frothy.

3 Heat a non-stick frying pan with a small amount of oil until the pan is very hot. Pour in just enough batter to cover the base of the pan, swirling the pan to cover the base evenly.

4 Cook until the pancake is set and golden, and then turn to cook the other side. Remove to a sheet of kitchen paper and then cook the remaining batter, to make about eight pancakes.

5 For the filling, drain the cherries, reserving the juice. Blend about 30ml/2 tbsp of the juice from the can of cherries with the arrowroot in a saucepan. Stir in the rest of the juice. Heat gently, stirring, until boiling. Stir over a moderate heat for about 2 minutes, until thickened and clear.

6 Add the cherries to the sauce and stir until thoroughly heated. Spoon the cherries into the pancakes and fold them into quarters.

Cook's Tip
If fresh cherries are in season, cook them gently in enough apple juice just to cover them, and then thicken the juice with arrowroot as in Step 5. The basic pancakes will freeze very successfully between layers of kitchen paper or greaseproof paper.

APRICOT AND ORANGE ROULADE

This elegant dessert is very good served with a spoonful of natural yogurt or crème fraîche.

INGREDIENTS

Serves 6
4 egg whites
115g/4oz/½ cup golden caster sugar
50g/2oz/½ cup plain flour
finely grated rind of 1 small orange
45ml/3 tbsp orange juice
10ml/2 tsp icing sugar and shreds of
    orange zest, to decorate

For the filling
115g/4oz/⅔ cup ready-to-eat dried
    apricots
150ml/¼ pint/⅔ cup orange juice

NUTRITION NOTES

Per portion:
Energy	203Kcals/853kJ
Fat	10.52g
Saturated fat	2.05g
Cholesterol	0
Fibre	2.53g

1 Preheat the oven to 200°C/400°F/ Gas 6. Grease a 23 x 33cm/9 x 13 in Swiss roll tin and line it with non-stick baking paper. Grease the paper.

2 For the roulade, place the egg whites in a large bowl and whisk them until they hold soft peaks. Gradually add the sugar, whisking hard between each addition.

3 Fold in the flour, orange rind and juice. Spoon the mixture into the prepared tin and spread it evenly.

4 Bake for about 15–18 minutes, or until the sponge is firm and light golden in colour. Turn out on to a sheet of non-stick baking paper and roll it up Swiss roll-style loosely from one short side. Leave to cool.

5 For the filling, roughly chop the apricots, and place them in a saucepan with the orange juice. Cover the pan and leave to simmer until most of the liquid has been absorbed. Purée the apricots in a food processor or blender.

6 Unroll the roulade and spread with the apricot mixture. Roll up, arrange strips of paper diagonally across the roll, sprinkle lightly with lines of icing sugar, remove the paper and scatter with orange zest to serve.

COOK'S TIP
Make and bake the sponge mixture a day in advance and keep it, rolled with the paper, in a cool place. Fill it with the fruit purée 2–3 hours before serving. The sponge can also be frozen for up to 2 months; thaw it at room temperature and fill it as above.

SUNFLOWER SULTANA SCONES

INGREDIENTS

Makes 10–12

225g/8oz/2 cups self-raising flour
5ml/1 tsp baking powder
25g/1oz/2 tbsp soft sunflower
  margarine
30ml/2 tbsp golden caster sugar
50g/2oz/⅓ cup sultanas
30ml/2 tbsp sunflower seeds
150g/5oz/⅔ cup natural yogurt
about 30–45ml/2–3 tbsp skimmed milk

1 Preheat the oven to 230°C/450°F/ Gas 8. Lightly oil a baking sheet. Sift the flour and baking powder into a bowl and rub in the margarine evenly.

2 Stir in the sugar, sultanas and half the sunflower seeds, then mix in the yogurt, with just enough milk to make a fairly soft, but not sticky dough.

3 Roll out on a lightly floured surface to about 2cm/¾ in thickness. Cut into 6cm/2½ in flower shapes or rounds with a biscuit cutter and lift on to the baking sheet.

4 Brush with milk and sprinkle with the reserved sunflower seeds, then bake for 10–12 minutes, until well risen and golden brown.

5 Cool the scones on a wire rack. Serve split and spread with jam or low fat spread.

NUTRITION NOTES	
Per portion:	
Energy	176Kcals/742kJ
Fat	5.32g
Saturated fat	0.81g
Cholesterol	0.84mg
Fibre	1.26g

PRUNE AND PEEL ROCK BUNS

INGREDIENTS

Makes 12

225g/8oz/2 cups plain flour
10ml/2 tsp baking powder
75g/3oz/⅔ cup demerara sugar
50g/2oz/½ cup chopped ready-to-eat
  dried prunes
50g/2oz/⅓ cup chopped mixed peel
finely grated rind of 1 lemon
50ml/2 fl oz/¼ cup sunflower oil
75ml/5 tbsp skimmed milk

NUTRITION NOTES	
Per portion:	
Energy	135Kcals/570kJ
Fat	3.35g
Saturated fat	0.44g
Cholesterol	0.13mg
Fibre	0.86g

1 Preheat the oven to 200°C/400°F/ Gas 6. Lightly oil a large baking sheet. Sift together the flour and baking powder, then stir in the sugar, prunes, peel and lemon rind.

2 Mix the oil and milk, then stir into the mixture, to make a dough which just binds together.

3 Spoon into rocky heaps on the baking sheet and bake for 20 minutes, until golden. Cool on a wire rack.

SAFFRON FOCCACIA

A dazzling yellow bread with a
distinctive flavour.

INGREDIENTS

Makes 1 loaf
pinch of saffron threads
150ml/¼ pint/⅔ cup boiling water
225g/8oz/2 cups plain flour
2.5ml/½ tsp salt
5ml/1 tsp easy-blend dried yeast
15ml/1 tbsp olive oil

For the topping
2 garlic cloves, sliced
1 red onion, cut into thin wedges
rosemary sprigs
*12 black olives, stoned and coarsely
    chopped*
15ml/1 tbsp olive oil

NUTRITION NOTES

Per loaf:
Energy	1047Kcals/4399kJ
Fat	29.15g
Saturated fat	4.06g
Cholesterol	0
Fibre	9.48g

1 Place the saffron in a heatproof jug
and pour on the boiling water.
Leave to infuse until the saffron mixture is lukewarm.

2 Place the flour, salt, yeast and olive
oil in a food processor. Turn on and
gradually add the saffron and its liquid
until the dough forms a ball.

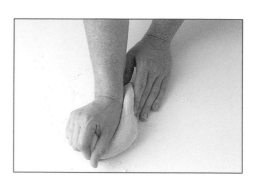

3 Turn out on to a floured board and
knead for 10–15 minutes. Place in a
bowl, cover and leave to rise for about
30–40 minutes, until doubled in size.

4 Punch down the risen dough on a
lightly floured surface and roll out
into an oval shape, 1cm/½ in thick.
Place on a lightly greased baking sheet
and leave to rise for 20–30 minutes.

5 Preheat the oven to 200°C/400°F/
Gas 6. Use your fingers to press
small indentations in the dough.

6 Cover with the topping ingredients,
brush lightly with olive oil, and
bake for about 25 minutes or until the
loaf sounds hollow when tapped on the
bottom. Leave to cool.

TOMATO BREADSTICKS

Once you've tried this simple recipe you'll never buy manufactured breadsticks again. Serve as a snack, or with aperitifs and a dip at the beginning of a meal.

INGREDIENTS

Makes 16
225g/8oz/2 cups plain flour
2.5ml/½ tsp salt
2.5ml/½ tbsp easy-blend dry yeast
5ml/1 tsp honey
5ml/1 tsp olive oil
150ml/¼ pint/⅔ cup warm water
6 halves sun-dried tomatoes in olive oil, drained and chopped
15ml/1 tbsp skimmed milk
10ml/2 tsp poppy seeds

NUTRITION NOTES

Per portion:

Energy	82Kcals/346kJ
Fat	3.53g
Saturated fat	0.44g
Cholesterol	0
Fibre	0.44g

1 Place the flour, salt and yeast in a food processor. Add the honey and olive oil and, with the machine running, gradually pour in the water (you may not need it all as flours vary). Stop adding water as soon as the dough starts to cling together. Process for 1 minute more.

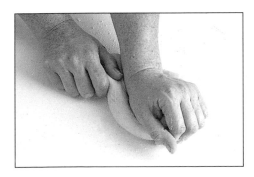

2 Turn out the dough on to a floured board and knead for 3–4 minutes until springy and smooth.

3 Knead in the chopped sun-dried tomatoes. Form into a ball and place in a lightly oiled bowl. Leave to rise for 5 minutes.

4 Preheat the oven to 150°C/300°F/Gas 2. Divide the dough into sixteen pieces and roll each piece into a 28 x 1cm/11 x ½ in long stick. Place on a lightly oiled baking sheet and leave to rise in a warm place for 15 minutes.

5 Brush the sticks with milk and sprinkle with poppy seeds. Bake for 30 minutes. Leave to cool on a wire cooling rack.

VARIATION
Instead of sun-dried tomatoes, you could try making these breadsticks with reduced fat Cheddar cheese, sesame seeds or herbs.

INDEX

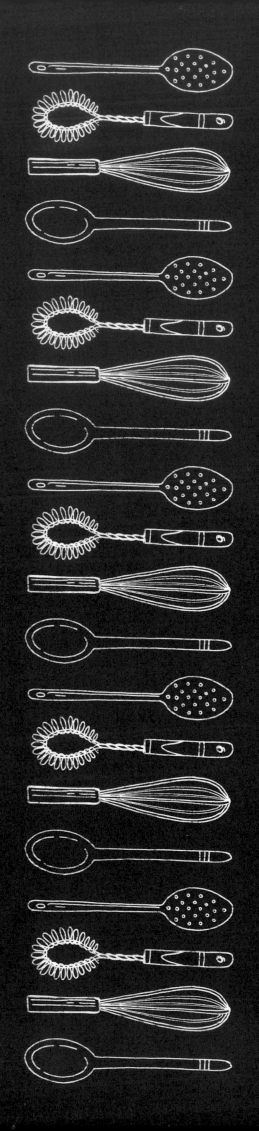